ENVIRONMENTAL RISK
AND THE PRESS

ENVIRONMENTAL RISK AND THE PRESS

An Exploratory Assessment

Peter M. Sandman
David B. Sachsman
Michael R. Greenberg
Michael Gochfeld

Transaction Books
New Brunswick (U.S.A.) and Oxford (U.K.)

070.44
S31-e

Library of Congress Catalog Number: 87-10849
ISBN 0-88738-172-3
Printed in the United States of America

Library of Congress Cataloging in Publication Data

Environmental risk and the press.

1. Environmental impact analysis. 2. Risk
management. 3. Reporters and reporting.
I. Sandman, Peter M.
TD194.6.E648 1987   070.4'493637   87-10849
ISBN 0-88738-172-3

Contents

List of Tables

Preface

The Environmental Risk Reporting Project is a joint effort of Rutgers—The State University of New Jersey, and the University of Medicine and Dentistry of New Jersey—Robert Wood Johnson Medical School. It is supported as a project of the National Science Foundation Industry/University Cooperative Center for Research in Hazardous and Toxic Substances, at the New Jersey Institute of Technology, an Advanced Technology Center of the New Jersey Commission on Science and Technology. The authors are principal investigators of this project along with Audrey R. Gotsch of UMDNJ—Robert Wood Johnson Medical School, and Mayme Jurkat of the Stevens Institute of Technology.

The authors first wish to thank the Industry/University Cooperative Center for Research in Hazardous and Toxic Substances, without whose support none of this research would have been possible, and our co-principal investigators, Professors Gotsch and Jurkat, who contributed to all aspects of the project.

This book reports the results of two related studies, an analysis of environmental risk reporting in New Jersey newspapers (Phase One) and a feasibility study for providing environmental risk information to the media (Phase Two). The two are inextricably tied: Phase One explores how the press covers environmental risk, while Phase Two explores what can be done to improve the coverage. To get an overall picture of this work, one should first read the Introduction, and then turn to the final chapter of this book, which contains a summary of this research as well as the project's conclusions.

These two studies are part of an ongoing research program undertaken by the Environmental Risk Reporting Project and its companion project, Risk Communication for Environmental News Sources. Among the other products of this research are: (1) "Covering An Environmental Accident," a videotape on how to cover a toxic spill, designed for journalists and journalism students; (2) *The Environmental News Source: Informing the Media During an Environmental Crisis*, a report on source–reporter interactions during emergencies, designed for technical and managerial people likely to be called upon as sources; (3) a bibliography on environ-

ix

mental risk communications (available September 1987); and (4) a content analysis of television network coverage of environmental risk (available January 1988). For more information on the work of the project, write Environmental Risk Reporting Project, Department of Journalism and Mass Media, Rutgers—The State University of New Jersey, New Brunswick, NJ 08903.

The authors wish to thank the following people for assistance in the Phase One research reported here: Judy Rankins and Cheryl DeSiena, for assistance in obtaining the archive articles; Cathy McDermott, for organizing the archive; Barbara Kwasnik, for content analysis coding; Alissa Bernholc, for the data analysis programming; Laurel Van Leer, for assistance with the expert analysis; Jim Detjen, Jim Lanard, Eugene Murphy, and Jim Sederis, for spending a grueling weekend reading and discussing the archive; and the editors, librarians, environmental reporters, and others at New Jersey's twenty–six daily newspapers, for selecting and providing the articles in the archive.

For their assistance in Phase Two research, the authors thank: Susan Sachs, for developing the Environmental Risk Reporting Survey of Reporters; Laurel Van Leer, for conducting the Phase Two interviews and for preparing a preliminary Phase Two report; Jim Detjen, for assisting in the survey development; Richard Skelly, for identifying the equipment needed, and costs involved, for the various options investigated in Phase Two; many sources in industry, government and environmental groups, for offering their advice on the best ways to provide risk information to the media; and reporters and editors across New Jersey, for telling us exactly what sort of help they want and need.

The authors also wish to thank B.J. Hance for preparing the Phase One and Phase Two report manuscripts; Kandice Salomone for preparing and editing the book manuscript; and Norma Reiss and Marsha Bergman, for secretarial support throughout the Project.

Introduction

The problems of New Jersey are the problems of America, only more so. Historically, New Jersey was among the first states to urbanize and among the first to industrialize. For many years, it was the prototypical American state. As recently as 1950, while more than one quarter of its residents lived in its six biggest cities, the Garden State still boasted of 26,900 farms. Since that time, New Jersey has transformed itself into the most suburban of American states, with only one–eighth of its 7.3 million residents living in the six cities that were once population centers, and only 9,100 farms.

Today, New Jersey has more people and more jobs per square mile than any other state in the nation. One reason for this is the state's history of industrialization. The density of industrial plants that border the New Jersey Turnpike is a testament to the continuing importance of industry to the state's economy. However, industry has created both prosperity and a long history of environmental risks to the public. By the Civil War, lead production had already contaminated the Raritan Bay, which lies between Northern New Jersey and Staten Island.

Currently, New Jersey is one of three states that lead the nation in the production of chemicals, and it has the greatest number of Superfund cleanup sites within its borders. The proximity of people to environmental hazards has created the potential for serious public health risks. The problem of environmental risk faces every state in the nation, but it faces New Jersey most starkly.

It is useful to study the "garden state" because New Jersey is not only a leader in environmental pollution, but also in public awareness of environmental risk. The people of New Jersey, the media that inform them, the state and local government officials, and the industries of the region agree on one thing—New Jersey has serious environmental risk problems that *are* taken seriously. The cleanup of hazardous waste sites was *the* major issue in the 1984 gubernatorial campaign. In 1981 and 1986 New Jersey voters overwhelmingly supported bond issues earmarked for the cleanup of toxic waste. The Garden State has some of the toughest environmental laws in the country.

This high degree of public awareness and concern for the environment makes New Jersey an ideal case study for determining the extent and effectiveness of environmental risk reporting in the mass media. Along with New Jersey's unwanted distinction as a leader in environmental pollution comes the transmission of large amounts of environmental news.

Since the mid-1970s, scarcely a news day has gone by in New Jersey without a local, regional, or national report of an environmental risk issue. Toxic spills, landfill leachate seeping into the groundwater of a community, acid rain, unacceptable air quality around the state's industrial centers—these are just a few of the stories that seem to break daily.

For most citizens, the environmental issues that are most important are those that they perceive as potentially affecting their health or safety, that is, issues of environmental risk. To find the information they need in order to make decisions about environmental risk—whether to oppose a local landfill, whether to put a charcoal filter on their tap, whether to vote for a candidate who promises to clean up the abandoned factory near their children's playground—people read the newspaper. Television in New Jersey is dominated by the New York and Philadelphia stations, leaving the newspaper as the state's principal source of local environmental news. How the state's newspapers cover environmental risk is therefore critical to public understanding, public attitudes, public fears, and ultimately public policy toward environmental risk in New Jersey.

There are probably very few reporters on New Jersey's twenty-six daily newspapers who have not covered an environmental story at some point in their tenure. If the subject of environmental risk came up—as it inevitably must in a situation such as a chemical leak or spill, a landfill siting, or a warehouse fire—these reporters found themselves in a maze of chemical nomenclature, health standards, and toxicological data. While some dailies have specialized reporters whose specific task is to cover the environment, many do not. And specialists may have nearly as difficult a time as their colleagues in dealing with and reporting the complexities of environmental risk issues. Since it is essential that the public be informed about environmental risk, and since the issues of environmental risk are complex and difficult to unravel, environmental news coverage is a vitally important and enormously challenging job for the media.

While the most fundamental problem characteristic of environmental news reporting is that environmental risk information is neither easy to obtain nor easy to understand, especially for a reporter working against a tight deadline, another problem is the uneasy relationship that has long existed between scientists and journalists. For these and other reasons, the quality of the coverage of today's complex environmental issues has often been a problem—for the reporters and editors, for industry and government, for environmentalists, and for citizens.

Phase One

Phase One of the Environmental Risk Reporting Project sought to evaluate the strengths and weaknesses of New Jersey's most professional environmental risk stories by collecting the "best" environmental risk articles published in 1984. These stories were selected by the editors of the twenty-six New Jersey daily newspapers as representing their five "best" stories on environmental risk. The collection of articles—hereafter referred to as "the archive"—was used for the analysis of the strengths and weaknesses of the state's most professional environmental risk reporting. Such an analysis is valuable in three ways. First, it can help reporters and editors decide how to upgrade the quality of their work—especially in the smaller media but even in the large dailies seeking to maintain their strengths and remedy their weaknesses. Second, it should interest scholars in journalism, environmental management, medicine, and related fields concerned with news source–media interactions, and sources who have an occasion to explain risk to the media—as a measure of the quality of the best environmental reporting from a state with some of the most serious environmental problems and some of the most skilled environmental reporters. Third, it provides the Environmental Risk Reporting Project with baseline information needed to determine which educational and informational efforts would be most useful for improving environmental risk reporting.

The analysis of the archive took two forms, a formal content analysis and a more subjective expert analysis. A formal content analysis—an objective, systematic, and quantitative description of content—relies on frequency counts of carefully defined dimensions. It has the advantages of consistency and lack of bias, since its assessments are not dependent on the viewpoints of those doing the assessing. It is limited, however, to those characteristics that can reliably be counted or measured. As an independent standard of environmental risk reporting, the expert analysis explicitly sought the evaluations of experts chosen to represent different views. Very different than formal content analysis, this approach constitutes a richer source of ideas, opinions, and assessments, and a useful measure of how experts define adequate reporting of environmental risk.

The content analysis focused on two principal characteristics of the archive: The first characteristic was source—how much of the information in the archive was provided by state officials, how much by industry sources, how much by environmentalists, and so on for thirteen types of sources. The second characteristic was approach to risk—how much of the archive asserted or denied that a particular situation was risky, how much assumed risk and asserted or denied that the situation was occurring, and so on for seven categories of risk approach. The unit of analysis was basically the paragraph, but other data—story length, hard news versus feature, etc.— were collected at the article level of analysis.

For the expert subjective analysis, four experts from four different fields were asked to review and discuss the archive in light of several standards, including objectivity, accuracy, writing quality, treatment of risk assessment variables, tone, newsworthiness, and enterprise. As opposed to the formal content analysis, the expert analysis was done on an article–by–article basis, with discussions generally centering on one of the variables mentioned above at a time. The experts concluded their analysis with an overall evaluation of the archive's strengths and weaknesses, and made recommendations based on their findings.

Based on the results of Phase One, the Environmental Risk Reporting Project concluded that much of the information the public needs to make decisions about environmental risk is not getting into newspapers. Results from the content analysis and the expert analysis confirmed each other by finding that information on environmental risk was lacking in newspaper coverage of the environment. The members of the expert panel, a journalist, a scientist, an industry representative, and an activist, had remarkably similar impressions of the archive in spite of their different perspectives on environmental issues (please refer to chapter 3):

> Overall, I have found very little risk reporting in the hundreds of articles we looked at. With few exceptions . . . most reporters just don't discuss risk.
>
> *Journalist*

> As a group, we seemed to feel that the treatment of risk left a great deal to be desired. The risk created by an environmental incident to human health and/ or the environment is what it's all about. How the risk is coped with, controlled, or eliminated makes the news.
>
> *Scientist*

> There was a woeful lack, in almost all cases, of an effort to measure what the hazard meant—the risk assessment question. . . .
>
> *Industry representative*

> Surprisingly, there was very little meaningful environmental risk reporting in the archive. I had expected to read a good deal about the risks associated . . . with a leak or a spill. As it turns out, I didn't read very much about risk.
>
> *Activist*

Phase Two

Based on the results of Phase One, the goal of the second phase was twofold: (1) to discover *why* environmental risk information is not getting into environmental news stories—especially first-day breaking stories; and

(2) to investigate the feasibility of various vehicles for getting environmental risk information to reporters and, ultimately, into their newspapers, especially into their coverage of environmental risk emergencies.

To find the answers to these questions, the Environmental Risk Reporting Project conducted surveys—by telephone, by mail, and in person at the Environmental Risk Reporting Symposium on October 4, 1985—with reporters from the twenty-six daily newspapers in New Jersey. Responses were also sought from industry representatives, local health officers, emergency response personnel, environmental activists, academic scientists, and government officials.

Basically, respondents were asked to answer two types of questions that corresponded with the two goals of this research. The first dealt with reporters' overall attitudes about risk reporting: What kind of risk information did they think was important? Did they really want more detailed risk information? Would they use it if they had it? From what sources did they want it? Were they currently having problems getting risk information?

The second set of questions investigated the respondents' feelings about the various options the project suggested for making risk information more readily available, especially during crises. At the project's inception, a Mobile Environmental Risk Information Team, consisting of public health experts who would travel to the site of a breaking environmental story and give background information to reporters, was the single option being considered. As more information was gathered from reporters and others, more options were added: (1) a 24-hour hotline that would staff public health experts around the clock to answer reporters' called-in questions; (2) a "wire service" that would telex or telecopy fact sheets, press releases, or ready-to-use background stories and graphics on environmental risk situations directly to newsrooms; and (3) an environmental risk library of relevant reference books for each newsroom, with training on how to use it for at least one reporter per newsroom.

Later on the scene—growing out of suggestions and comments offered by reporters during interviews and at the Symposium—came the idea of an environmental risk press kit. The press kit would include the names and telephone numbers of sources of information from different fields, a glossary of technical terms, short essays by experts on strategies and problems of covering particular environmental situations, and other information that would be useful to reporters covering environmental risk stories—all presented in a form they were familiar with.

It is important to stress that the main concern of the research in Phase Two was how to provide more background information on risk for breaking news stories—that is, fires, chemical spills, and similar emergency situations. Some of the options considered later in the research (such as the telephone hotline) would also be useful to reporters working on chronic risk stories, background stories, features, and the like. Improving non–emergency coverage is of course valuable in its own right, but the focus of the Phase Two research was improving background risk information in breaking environmental news, and the options are evaluated chiefly in terms of their contribution to that goal.

To get an overall picture of the Phase One and Phase Two research, one may first want to read the final chapter of this book, the summary and conclusions, before reading the body of the text.

The conclusions based on both phases of this research represent not only the Environmental Risk Reporting Project's findings but also the thoughts of reporters and other professionals who were interviewed. The authors feel that only through this cooperation can environmental risk reporting achieve and maintain excellence.

PHASE ONE
EVALUATING ENVIRONMENTAL RISK REPORTING

1

The Archive of Environmental Risk Reporting

The Environmental Risk Reporting Project sought to evaluate the most professional reporting of environmental risk across the state of New Jersey by collecting and analyzing the best articles published in 1984 on the subject. It was the goal of the project to evaluate the best environmental risk reporting, not a cross–section, because the project wanted to match the risk content of the best stories against what experts think constitutes adequate reporting of environmental risk.

Collecting the Archive

To collect the archive, the editors of the twenty–six daily newspapers in New Jersey were each invited to send to the project five of their best articles (or series, special issues, or other "packages") dealing with environmental risk. The fact that the editors themselves chose what they considered to be the best articles assured a sound basis for evaluating the most professional environmental reporting in New Jersey.

All twenty–six newspapers submitted articles. For twenty–one of the twenty–six, the editor or his or her designee (often the newspaper's environmental reporter or its librarian) selected the articles for the archive. The articles were not picked by the project, nor were they chosen as bad examples. Five newspapers, rather than choosing articles themselves, invited the project to select articles on pollution, hazardous waste, the environment, etc. from their morgues. In these cases, to assure neutrality, project researchers photocopied many articles and then selected the five longest articles for the archive. The assumption was that the longest articles were likeliest to be the best.

In many cases editors did not submit five individual stories. A series (a number of articles appearing on the same topic on different days), a pack-

3

age (several different articles on the same topic on the same day, including sidebars), or a special section or supplement was counted as one "item" toward the total of five. Thus, a unit item could be either a twelve–paragraph article or a five–part series. (In the content analysis itself, each article was analyzed independently, not as part of an "item." There were 130 items, but nearly twice as many individual articles.)

Occasionally a newspaper sent more than five items. In this case, the articles which had nothing to do with environmental risk were eliminated first (for example, an article about a bond issue); then, of the remaining articles, the five longest items were chosen for the archive.

Articles that originated from a wire service were eliminated regardless of how many items were submitted. Also, no editorials, letters to the editor, or opinion columns were included in the archive. All articles were locally written and all were news.

Contents of the Archive

A total of 248 individual articles make up the archive. These contain 6486 paragraphs. There are eighty–eight (35%) single articles; ninety–eight (40%) articles that were part of packages (more than one article on the same day); five (2%) articles that were part of series (more than one article on different days); and fifty–seven (23%) articles that were both packages and series (more than one article on the same day, and more than one day). The length criterion for choosing items for the archive of course led to an overabundance of series, packages, and special sections as opposed to individual articles.

The minimum number of individual articles per newspaper in the archive is four (one paper); the maximum is forty–nine (one paper); the mode is five (nine papers). Of the twenty–six newspapers in the archive, twenty–two were represented by four to eight articles apiece; those with more than eight articles in the archive (because of multi–part packages or special sections) were the *Daily Advance*, the *Burlington County Times*, the *Asbury Park Press*, and the *News Tribune*.

The length of articles in the archive ranges from five paragraphs to 120 paragraphs; the median length is twenty–two paragraphs, and the mean length is twenty–six paragraphs.

Of the 248 articles in the archive, 112 (45%) were coded as hard news, 83 (33%) were features, 35 (14%) were background articles, 16 (6%) were investigative articles, and 2 (1%) were other.

Table 1.1 lists the twenty–six newspapers and their individual contributions to the archive. They are listed in descending order based on number of articles in the archive. Note that the *News Tribune* and the *Asbury Park*

TABLE 1.1
Contents of the Archive

Newspaper	Number of Articles	Number of Paragraphs
News Tribune	49	1053
Asbury Park Press	42	1132
Burlington County Times	17	686
Daily Advance	12	190
Ocean County Observer	8	354
Millville Daily	8	188
Gloucester County Times	8	169
Courier–News	7	205
Herald–News	6	244
Trenton Times	6	174
Home News	6	167
Daily Journal	6	161
New Jersey Herald	6	156
Vineland Times–Journal	6	144
Daily Record	6	110
The News	6	102
Record	5	280
Star–Ledger	5	186
Courier–Post	5	146
Daily Register	5	113
Bridgeton Evening News	5	105
Jersey Journal	5	99
Today's Sunbeam	5	86
Trentonian	5	83
Dispatch	5	72
The Press	4	81
Total	248	6486

Press are over–sampled because both submitted long special sections. While there is no reason to believe that this significantly affected the findings, the reader should bear in mind that the archive is not a probability sample of New Jersey newspaper coverage of environmental risk. It is, rather, a collection of articles submitted by the state's newspaper editors as samples of their best environmental risk reporting. The project's goal was to determine what was good and bad about the most professional environmental risk reporting available, not to judge the daily output of environmental news.

2

Content Analysis of the Environmental Risk Archive

The analysis of the archive began with a formal content analysis, an objective, systematic, and quantitative description of the content of the 248 environmental risk news stories. The formal content analysis focused on two characteristics of the archive: (1) Source, that is, where the information came from, and (2) Risk, or what the articles said about whether a substance or situation was risky or not risky, present or not present. The main unit of analysis was the paragraph; each paragraph was coded according to these two variables. In all, there were thirteen categories of sources, and seven categories of risk (risky, not risky, mixed opinion if risky, substance present, not present, mixed opinion if present, and no mention of risk).

Methods

The formal content analysis coding scheme was designed, pretested, and revised several times before an unbiased, reliable system was developed, but the two key variables, Source and Risk, remained the same throughout.

The coding scheme evolved in the following manner: First, the coding instructions were given to three naive (untrained) coders who read and discussed them to ensure they understood them. Then the coders separately coded several articles that were not part of the archive and calculated their intercoder reliability. The coders then discussed reasons for any difficulties in coding the articles and made suggestions for improvement of the coding system and instructions. New instructions were then written, and the process started from the beginning with new coders.

Intercoder reliability of the final method was 81% (that is, coders made the same judgment 81% of the time). The assessment of risk was somewhat less reliable than the assessment of source (75% reliability for risk as opposed to 87% reliability for source). These reliability levels were deemed satisfactory, and thereafter a single coder was employed to conduct the entire content analysis.

The final instruction sheet and coding form are contained in Appendix A. To summarize the coding procedure, however: The coder read the article to get a sense of its overall meaning. Then each paragraph in the article was numbered. The general information on the coding sheet was filled out for each article—the newspaper, headline, date, type of article (hard news, feature, etc.), and so on. With this information, the archive could be analyzed on an article–by–article level.

The coding sheet lists thirteen types of sources:

- Federal Government: United States Environmental Protection Agency (EPA), other federal agencies, members of Congress, etc.
- State Government: New Jersey Department of Environmental Protection (DEP), other state agencies and legislators.
- County Government: County health officers, sheriff's officers, other county officials.
- Local Government: Local police, firefighters, mayor, other local officials.
- Government General: Unspecified references to government, such as "officials," "inspectors," "authorities," etc., and mixtures of government levels.
- Industry and Industry Associations: Company officials and spokespeople, plant managers, and industry groups such as the Chemical Manufacturers Association.
- Workers and Unions: Individual workers, strikers, or union officials or spokespeople.
- Advocacy Groups: Local, state, or national organizations concerned with environmental risk issues, such as the Sierra Club, Public Interest Research Group, etc.
- Citizens: Residents, neighbors, or passers–by (those not connected with the story as a representative of one of the other sources).
- Experts: Experts (at a hospital or university, etc.) contacted by the reporter specifically for background or technical information.
- Unattributed: Summaries of what happened or reporters' observations which do not mention source.
- Mixed attribution: Several sources from different categories cited in the same paragraph.
- Other: Any other sources.

The key question for the risk part of the content analysis was whether a paragraph specifically addressed the presence or absence of a toxic substance or an environmental hazard, or whether it addressed the riskiness of a substance or hazard. For example, a paragraph on dioxin in a landfill story may focus on whether dioxin is dangerous (or how dangerous it is) or on whether there is dioxin in the landfill (or how much of it there is). A risk or presence paragraph, moreover, could take any of three positions on the issue: (1) risk–asserting or presence–asserting (it's dangerous or it's there); (2) risk–denying or presence–denying (it's not dangerous or it's not there); or (3) an intermediate, mixed, or uncertain position (it's somewhat dangerous, we're not sure if it's there, etc.). Each paragraph was coded only for its dominant risk content; since journalistic paragraphs are short, difficult–to–code combinations were rare. Thus, each paragraph was coded into one of seven categories: risky, not risky, can't tell if it's risky, hazard present, not present, can't tell if it's present, and no risk information.

For each numbered paragraph, the coder checked off one type of source and one risk category. A coding sheet was filled out for each article. Thus, each paragraph in every article in the archive was coded according to where the information came from and what it had to say about risk.

Only two problems of any significance were encountered in coding the archive. First, where documents were the source, they were coded under the source from which the document originated, even if that source did not willingly surrender the document. For example, a letter from industry that was uncovered by an advocacy group would be coded under industry. In retrospect, since this "source" was not voluntarily providing the information, a separate category for documents would have been preferable.

Second, there was no category for housing authorities, water control district representatives, and other regional government sources. These were therefore coded under "government general." This category thus consists of mixed government sources ("federal and state officials said"), unspecific government sources ("authorities said"), and regional government sources. A separate category for regional authorities would have been preferable.

Neither documents nor regional officials were quoted often enough to significantly alter the overall trends in source attributions.

Once the coding was completed, the information was entered into the computer for subsequent analysis.

Results

The coding of the archive permitted many different kinds of analyses on both the paragraph level and the article level. The most interesting and useful trends uncovered in the analysis of the data were the overall distribution of source and risk on both the paragraph and the article level, and the relationship between source and risk—that is, what specific sources said about risk, and where various kinds of risk information are coming from.

At the paragraph level, the project determined what percentage of all paragraphs in the archive cite a particular source, such as industry. Similarly, in the analysis on the article level, the project found what percentage of all articles include at least one paragraph citing industry. The distinction between these two levels of analysis is important to understanding the results that follow.

Overall Distribution of Sources

A crucial focus of the content analysis is what sources were relied on by reporters, and the "profile" of each source's approach to risk. In assessing these findings it is important to bear in mind that the patterns that emerge could result from at least six factors: (1) which sources make themselves available to reporters; (2) what the sources choose to say; (3) which sources reporters seek out for interviews; (4) what the reporters choose to ask; (5) what information reporters put in their stories; and (6) what information editors ask for, accept, or delete. Thus a finding that a particular source is frequently or infrequently cited, or that the source tends to assert or deny risk, may result from any combination of source behavior, reporter behavior, and editor behavior. Other research methods must be used to explain the patterns of coverage revealed by the content analysis.

Table 2.1 shows the overall distribution of sources by paragraph. The heavy reliance on government sources is the most significant finding of this

TABLE 2.1
Overall Distribution of Sources by Paragraph

Source	Number of Paragraphs that Mention Source*	Percent of All Paragraphs	Percent of Paragraphs excluding Unattributed
Federal Government	297	4.6%	7.0%
State Government	954	14.7	22.5
County Government	310	4.8	7.3
Local Government	479	7.4	11.3
Government General	360	5.6	8.5
Industry	636	9.8	15.0
Workers	99	1.5	2.3
Advocacy Groups	277	4.3	6.5
Citizens	306	4.7	7.2
Experts	274	4.2	6.5
Unattributed	2251	34.7	–
Mixed	227	3.5	5.4
Other	16	0.2	0.4

*Total number of paragraphs is 6,486.

analysis; 37.1% of the paragraphs in the archive cite the government. With the unattributed paragraphs eliminated, we see that 56.6% of the sources cited in the archive are government. State government is the most frequently cited (14.7%) of the various types of government sources, with the federal government cited the least (4.6%). Local government, cited in 7.4% of the paragraphs, is generally on the scene or easily accessible to the news media; hence, its relatively high visibility in the archive.

Unattributed paragraphs—statements which did not carry any reference—accounted for 34.7% of the material in the archive. Many of these are the reporter's firsthand observation of events; others are summaries and integrations of what the sources have said.

Among non–government sources, industry was the most frequently cited (9.8%). Advocacy groups, citizens, and experts received an intermediate amount of attention (4.3%, 4.7%, and 4.2% respectively), while workers were rarely used as sources (1.5%). The relatively low attention to experts is worth noting, since uninvolved experts are presumably the best sources of unbiased technical information about environmental risk. Also worth noting is the fairly low reliance on citizens, since it is often argued that environmental coverage relies too heavily on citizens, for example frightened people whose homes are near landfills. Advocacy groups might justly complain that they received less than half the attention accorded to industry, although the total of citizens and advocacy groups (9.0%) was about even with industry's contribution.

The distribution of sources on the article level is shown in Table 2.2. In 56.0% of the articles, the state government is cited at least once, which one would expect given the high number of paragraphs attributed to the state in the previous analysis. However, the number of articles that cite other forms of government at least once is higher relative to state government on the article level than on the paragraph level—25.4% for the federal government, 23.8% for the county, 38.7% for local government, and 36.3% for government–general. This means simply that although more paragraphs are devoted to what the state says, the typical article cites at least one other level of government as well.

On the article level, the presence of experts is more encouraging than the number of paragraphs devoted to them. In over one fourth of the articles (27.0%), experts were cited in at least one paragraph. Thus, although more space is being devoted to other sources, experts are not entirely ignored.

Workers fared a little better relative to industry on the article level. The number of paragraphs attributed to industry is about six times the number attributed to workers, but the number of articles in which industry is cited is only four times the number of articles that cited workers at least once.

As on the paragraph level, the total contributions of citizens (21.8%) and

TABLE 2.2
Overall Distribution of Sources by Article

Source	Number of Articles that Mention Source at Least Once*	Percent of All Articles
Federal Government	63	25.4%
State Government	139	56.0
County Government	59	23.8
Local Government	96	38.7
Government General	90	36.3
Industry	100	40.3
Workers	22	8.9
Advocacy Groups	47	19.0
Citizens	54	21.8
Experts	67	27.0
Unattributed	241	97.2
Mixed	67	27.0
Other	6	2.4

*Total number of articles is 248.

advocacy groups (19.0%) equalled industry attributions (40.3%) in the archive.

Totalling the figures in Table 2.2 (leaving out the "unattributed" category) and dividing the sum by the total number of articles in the archive, we see that the average article cited 3.3 sources.

Overall Distribution of Risk Approaches

The overall distribution of statements about risk on the paragraph level is shown in Table 2.3. More than two-thirds of all the paragraphs in the archive deal with other things besides environmental risk. This is not necessarily surprising in light of the fact that the articles have many other topics to cover, such as blame, cost, politics, and so on. It is nonetheless interesting that in articles selected as examples of environmental risk reporting, only one-third of the paragraphs actually discuss risk.

Of the third of the paragraphs that do discuss risk, roughly half (15.0%) deal with whether the presumably risky substance is present; only 17.4% of the paragraphs in the overall archive address the "pure" risk issue: how dangerous is this substance or situation?

Moreover, the majority of the risk-relevant paragraphs are more alarming than reassuring: they tend to assert risk (10.0%) rather than deny it

TABLE 2.3
Overall Distribution of Risk Approaches by Paragraph

Risk Category	Number of Paragraphs with Risk Approach*	Percent of All Paragraphs
Risky	650	10.0%
Not Risky	206	3.2
Mixed Opinion (if risky)	274	4.2
Risky Substance Present	662	10.2
Risky Substance Not Present	149	2.3
Mixed Opinion (if present)	161	2.5
No Risk Information	4384	67.6

*Total number of paragraphs is 6,486.

TABLE 2.4
Overall Distribution of Risk Approaches by Article

Risk Category	Number of Articles with Risk Approach at Least Once*	Percent of All Articles
Risky	142	57.3%
Not Risky	71	28.6
Mixed Opinion (if risky)	111	44.8
Risky Substance Present	159	64.1
Risky Substance not Present	68	27.4
Mixed Opinion (if present)	71	28.6
No Risk Information	247	99.6

Total number of articles is 248.

(3.2%), and they tend to say the risky substance is present (10.2%) rather than not present (2.3%). (This is not surprising since a non–risk situation is likely to be interpreted as a non–event and, therefore, not be covered at all. Whether the greater frequency of risk assertions than risk denials represents a journalistic imbalance is a hotly debated matter of opinion.)

Paragraphs that have mixed or intermediate views about risk and presence are not common, with 4.2% of the paragraphs in the middle about risk, and 2.5% in the middle about presence. This characteristic of the archive can be attributed in part to a convention of journalism: that the middle is achieved by contrasting both extremes rather than asserting the middle. Also, sources that adopt intermediate positions may be less likely to seek coverage than those on the extremes.

On the article level (Table 2.4), virtually every article has at least one paragraph that does not deal with risk. Over half (57.3%) of the articles have at least one paragraph that asserts riskiness, and nearly two–thirds of the articles have at least one paragraph that says the hazardous substance or situation is present. By contrast, only 28.6% of the articles contain a denial that the situation is risky, and only 27.4% of the articles have at least one paragraph that denies the situation is present. In short, in a majority of the articles there is nothing that says the situation is not dangerous or present. This, of course, does not necessarily mean the reporting is biased in any way; we cannot conclude from the archive whether the imbalance of risk assertions over risk denials accurately reflects what the available sources were saying, much less whether it accurately reflects environmental reality. We can conclude that the imbalance is a real characteristic of the archive. Alarming paragraphs and articles are substantially more common than reassuring ones.

The middle view occurs more often on the article level than on the paragraph level of analysis. In 44.8% of the articles, there is at least one paragraph that takes an intermediate position on risk; 28.6% of the articles have at least one paragraph expressing mixed feelings about presence.

In summary, it is quite common for an article to assert risk or presence, somewhat less common for an article to say it is not sure, and fairly uncommon for an article to deny risk or presence. However, even the number of assertions of risk seems rather low when one considers that the articles in the archive were submitted as examples of environmental risk reporting. It is possible that New Jersey editors responded to the request to send articles on environmental risk with articles concerning the environment in general, such as bond issues, landfill siting, etc. It is also possible that most articles on environmentally risky situations do not pay much attention to the details of risk assessment.

Distribution of Source and Risk Categories by Newspaper

Distribution of source and risk categories can also be examined on the newspaper level, that is, where are particular papers getting their information, and what do they have to say about risk. Due to the small size and non–randomness of the sample from each newspaper, these trends are very limited in usefulness and are presented only to give a sense of the variation in the archive.

Some newspapers in the archive were found to rely strongly on industry sources. The *Daily Advance*, for example, cited an industry source in 26.3% of its paragraphs, while workers and citizens were not cited at all, and advocacy groups only once. In the overall distribution of sources, the ratio of industry sources to citizens plus advocacy groups is about even; in this paper (for articles in the archive), the ratio is 50:1. Whereas the overall ratio of combined government sources to industry is approximately 4:1, in the *Daily Advance* sample, the ratio is less than 2:1, with ninety–one paragraphs that cite government sources to industry's fifty. County and local government were used as sources more frequently than the state, and the federal government was cited in none of the paragraphs. The trends for this newspaper are put into perspective by reviewing the individual articles it contributed to the archive, however. One item was a long article on food irradiation that reflected an industry point of view; the others were mainly about landfill closings and sitings—issues dealt with on a local government level.

Some newspapers had higher numbers of paragraphs in which advocacy groups and citizens were cited than other sources. For example, the *Courier–News* showed 21.0% of all paragraphs came from citizens and another 3.4% from advocacy groups. In contrast, only 7.8% of the paragraphs were attributed to industry sources, and 39.5% to combined government sources. There were other papers that had higher than the overall trend in citizen and advocacy group attributions relative to industry: the *Bridgeton Evening News* (21.9% citizens and advocacy groups combined, 0.0% industry), *The Daily Register* (13.3% citizens and advocacy groups, 0.9% industry), *The Star–Ledger* (16.7% citizens and advocacy groups, 2.7% industry), the *Gloucester County Times* (12.4% citizens and advocacy groups, 3.6% industry), and the *Asbury Park Press* (13.1% citizens and advocacy groups, 5.8% industry) among others.

On the other hand, some papers were high in government attributions. The *Home News*, for example, showed a total of 127 or 76.1% of its paragraphs from government sources, as opposed to four paragraphs from all other sources combined (36 paragraphs were unattributed). The *Trenton Times* cited the state government in 35.0% of its paragraphs. Attributions to experts were high in some newspapers—the *Courier–Post* (13.7%) and *The Press* (21.0%) were highest—but most newspapers had few if any expert attributions.

So, at least for this small sample of the "best" environmental risk stories, there is a variation in the sources used by newspapers.

Similar trends exist in the distribution of risk statements among the twenty–six newspapers. There is an enormous range in the percentage of paragraphs in the archive that assert an environmental situation is risky, from none in *Today's Sunbeam* to 38.1% in the *Ocean County Observer*.

The mean for all paragraphs that assert risk in all newspapers is 9.5%. There are several papers at the low extreme and several at the high extreme. The trends for risk denials were similar, although there were five papers that had no risk–denying statements. For mixed statements about risk, the numbers were again varied, but one paper, *The Press*, had an extremely high number of mixed statements about presence (21.0% versus the mean of 3.13%). (Interestingly, this paper also had the highest number of expert attributions. Although the findings show that mixed positions about risk in the archive do not as a rule come from experts, this particular paper, at least, seems to reflect the stereotype of experts taking the middle ground.)

Obviously, the overall archive is influenced more heavily by the three papers that contributed the highest number of paragraphs to the archive (*Asbury Park Press*, 1132; *News Tribune*, 1053; *Burlington County Times*, 686). While every newspaper's articles were unique to some extent, the contributions of these three yielded means close to the overall archive means, suggesting that their overrepresentation does not significantly distort the archive findings.

Relationship between Source and Risk Approach

The most interesting and relevant data afforded by the analysis of the archive is the relationship between sources and statements about risk. That is, are paragraphs from industry sources, for example, more likely to deny the risk than to assert it? Or, to consider the same data from a different perspective, are paragraphs that deny the risk more likely to come from industry than from, say, advocacy groups?

WHAT DOES EACH SOURCE SAY ABOUT RISK? Table 2.5 shows what each kind of source said about risk in the articles. The following discussion will be on a source–by–source basis; the percentages given represent the percentage of all paragraphs a particular source contributed to the archive; each horizontal row in Table 2.5 sums to 100.0%. For example, the statement "local government says risk is present 5.2% of the time" means that of all paragraphs attributed to local government, 5.2% of them say the risk was present. After this, the data will be reviewed one risk category at a time to see which sources are contributing the information in each risk category.

Federal government. When the federal government is cited about risk, it tends to be more on the subject of whether the situation is present than whether the situation is risky. In the paragraphs attributed to the federal government, 20.8% discuss the presence of hazardous situations (versus 15.0% for all sources). Like most sources, the federal government is four times more likely to say a hazard is present (12.8%) than not present

TABLE 2.5
Percentage of Paragraphs of Each Source to Each Risk Approach
(horizontal rows sum to 100%)

Source	Risky (%)	Not Risky (%)	Mixed Opinion (if Risky) (%)	Risky Substance Present (%)	Risky Sub. Not Present (%)	Mixed Opinion (if present) (%)	No Risk Info (%)
Federal Government	7.1	5.4	3.7	12.8	3.0	5.0	63.0
State Government	10.2	1.9	5.6	11.5	1.8	3.8	65.3
County Government	6.4	0.6	1.6	8.1	1.3	3.5	78.4
Local Government	7.9	6.3	4.4	5.2	2.9	3.8	69.5
Government General	8.6	6.9	5.8	7.8	1.7	1.4	67.8
Industry	1.6	8.2	2.7	8.6	7.5	2.2	69.2
Workers	15.1	9.1	12.1	22.2	0.0	0.0	41.4
Advocacy Groups	13.4	0.4	6.1	11.2	1.8	0.7	66.4
Citizens	16.3	3.6	7.5	12.4	2.6	4.2	53.2
Experts	21.2	6.9	5.8	11.7	4.7	3.6	46.0
Unattributed	6.4	0.5	2.8	11.0	0.9	1.5	76.9
Mixed	56.8	4.8	6.6	4.0	2.2	1.3	24.2
Other	0.0	0.0	0.0	12.5	0.0	0.0	87.5
Average for all Sources	10.0	3.2	4.2	10.2	2.3	2.5	67.6

(3.0%). In 5.0% of the paragraphs (twice the overall average), the federal government is in the middle on presence.

When cited on risk, the federal government says a situation is risky (7.1%) more often than not (5.4%), and cannot tell 3.7% of the time. However, it is less likely than the overall (10.0%) to assert riskiness, and it denies riskiness more often than the overall average (3.2%). The federal government is thus a relatively reassuring source.

State government. The state government is equally likely to be cited on both risk (17.7%) and presence (17.1%). However, there are many more paragraphs from the state that say a situation is risky (10.2%) or present (11.5%) than there are assertions that a situation is not risky (1.9%) or not present (1.8%). Compared to the overall, the state is more likely to have a mixed opinion on both risk (5.6% state, 4.2% overall) and presence (3.8% state, 2.5% overall).

Relative to the overall averages, the state is slightly more likely to assert risk, less likely to deny risk, and more likely to take a middle position. Compared to other sources, the state is more likely to say a hazard is present, and less likely to deny presence. It also has a mixed opinion more often than the average.

Since the state is the largest source in the archive aside from unattributed sources, contributing 14.7% of all paragraphs, it is significant that the state's overall message in the archive is an assertion of both presence and risk. Though the state often adopts middle positions, an important and responsible role for state government sources, on the alarming–versus–reassuring dimension this dominant and highly credible source is generally on the alarming side.

County government. The county government, compared to the overall, is less often cited about both risk and presence (except the middle position on presence). Its high proportion of no–risk–information paragraphs (78.4% versus 67.6% overall) suggests that the county government is used on the scene to answer questions about what happened, and can be easily reached for quotes about other issues (landfill siting, bond issues), but that it is not heavily relied on for risk information. When the county is cited about risk, however, it is far more likely to say a situation is risky (6.4%) or present (8.1%) than not risky (0.6%) or not present (1.3%).

Local government. Local government is slightly higher than the overall average in paragraphs about risk, and considerably lower in paragraphs about presence. When cited on either topic it is more likely than the overall average to be on the reassuring side. Local government denies risk nearly twice as often as the overall average (6.3% to 3.2%), and nearly as often as it asserts risk (7.9%). Although the local government is cited less frequently than the overall on whether a hazard is present, when cited it is less likely to assert presence, more likely to deny presence, and more likely to say it cannot tell. It is the most reassuring of government sources.

General government. The general government category ("officials say") has a higher than average number of paragraphs attributed to it on the subject of riskiness (21.3% general government, 17.4% overall), and a lower than average attention to presence (10.9% to 15.0%). When "officials" are cited, they are below the average in assertions of risk and above it in risk denials and mixed opinions/cannot tell; thus they are a comparatively reassuring source. When general government sources are cited about whether a hazard is present, they are (like the averages) much more likely to say that it is present (7.8%) than it is not (1.7%) or they cannot tell (1.4%).

Industry. Industry is less likely than all other sources except county government to be cited on risk. When industry does talk about risk, however, it says "not risky" more than any other group except workers (8.2% industry, 9.1% workers) and more than twice as often as the average (3.2%). Unlike workers, moreover, industry very seldom asserts risk, less often than any other source. Only 1.6% of the paragraphs attributed to industry assert risk, as opposed to the overall average of 10.0%. Industry is thus the only source in the archive to deny risk more often than it asserts risk.

While industry confirms presence (8.6%) more than it denies it (7.5%), it confirms less often than the overall average, and denies far more often than the overall average. Mixed opinion/cannot tell paragraphs for industry are below average for both risk and presence.

Industry's high denials of risk and presence are particularly interesting in light of the number of paragraphs in the archive that come from that source. Leaving aside unattributed sources, industry is second only to the state in number of paragraphs, contributing 9.8% of the archive.

Workers. Workers are interesting and surprising sources. They are the least frequently cited source, but when cited they are the most likely of any source to address the issues of risk and presence; that is, they are far below the overall average for no–risk–information paragraphs (41.4% versus 67.6% overall). Most likely because of their positions in companies that may be creating environmental situations, workers are ambivalent about risk. Of the 36.3% of the paragraphs in which workers are cited about risk, 15.1% say it is risky, 9.1% say it is not, and 12.1% say they cannot tell. Workers deny risk and adopt an intermediate position on risk more than any other source, far more than the average. However, they are also well above the overall figure for risk assertion; in fact they are the fourth highest for risk assertion, behind mixed sources, experts, and citizens.

On the issue of presence, workers always say the hazardous substance is present; 22.2% of the worker paragraphs assert presence while no paragraphs deny presence or take a middle position. The 22.2% figure is double the overall average and considerably higher than for any other source. Bear in mind that workers constitute a very small portion of the archive, contributing 1.5% of the total number of paragraphs in 8.9% of the articles. Workers may be interviewed chiefly in situations where there is an obvious risk, like a spill or a fire, and are probably not sought out as sources for other issues. The small number of worker attributions also means the interpretation of this group's data must be tentative; a small number of stories could greatly affect the figures.

Advocacy groups. Advocacy groups are in about the middle of the pack for citations about risk and presence, a little above average on risk and a little below average on presence. When they are cited on risk, advocacy groups assert the risk (13.4%) or have a mixed opinion about it (6.1%), but very seldom deny it (0.4%). In fact, advocacy groups deny risk less frequently than any other source. Along the same lines, advocacy groups nearly always confirm the presence of the hazardous substance or situation (11.2%) rather than deny it (1.8%) or have mixed feelings (0.7%).

Advocacy groups are another relatively small group of sources, contributing only 4.3% of the total paragraphs in the archive. But when added together with citizens—the rationale being that advocacy groups are citizens who have organized—their contribution doubles, since citizens also tend to confirm presence and riskiness.

Citizens. Private citizens are the fourth highest source for citations about risk, the third highest for citations about presence, and above the average in both categories. Most of the time, they are saying that something is risky (16.3%) or present (12.4%). Less frequently, but still more than the average for all sources, they are saying they cannot tell if something is risky (7.5%) or present (4.2%). Far less often do they say something is not risky (3.6%) or not present (2.6%). But citizens are so far below the average for no–risk–information paragraphs (53.2% versus 67.6% overall) that they are above the overall average even for risk denials. Thus it is not accurate to charge that citizens are quoted by the media almost exclusively to assert risk. The ratio of alarming to reassuring to intermediate citations for citizens roughly parallels the ratio for all sources.

Citizens are cited in the archive only slightly more often than advocacy groups (4.7% of paragraphs), but, as pointed out previously, there is some rationale for combining citizen sources and advocacy group sources for the sake of this discussion. Doing this raises the overall contribution of citizens and advocacy groups to 9.0% of the total number of paragraphs.

It is important to bear in mind that the types of risk statements that come from citizens are coded the same as risk statements that come from other sources. For example, a citizen saying "I live next door and I know there's some rotten stuff there," or "I've lived here all my life and I'm confident that it's safe" is coded the same as a government official reporting test results. Possible differences in the impact of these types of statements are discussed further in the subjective analysis.

Experts. Experts say a situation is risky more frequently than any other source except "mixed" (21.2%), and more than twice as much as the overall average. They deny risk frequently also (6.9%), again more than twice the overall average. They present a mixed opinion somewhat less (5.8%), though still more than the overall figure. They are modestly above the overall average in asserting presence (11.7%), and more than double the average in denying presence (4.7%), which they do more than any other source except industry. Experts are relatively high also in mixed opinions about whether a risk is present (3.6%).

Thus experts are above average in all six categories of risk information, and comparably below average in no–risk–information paragraphs (46.0% versus 67.6%). This is predictable, since uninvolved experts are more likely to be asked about risk than about other aspects of the story such as blame and cost. What was not so predictable is the finding that expert citations were about as alarming as citations from other sources, and more likely than citations from other sources to take a definite stand. The image of experts as inclined to reassure or to temporize is not borne out in the archive. Citizens, in the archive, tended unexpectedly toward the middle position on risk; experts tended unexpectedly toward the extremes.

Experts are not, however, given much attention in the archive, quoted in only 4.2% of the total paragraphs—slightly less than either citizens or advocacy groups. Viewed on the article level, however, 27.0% of all articles have at least one paragraph attributed to an expert.

Unattributed. As could be expected, unattributed sources are relatively high in the no–risk–information category (76.9%), which accounts for background material and firsthand reporting of events not directly related to risk. Unattributed paragraphs on risk are more scarce than unattributed paragraphs on presence, though both are below the overall averages.

Unattributed paragraphs are more likely to say something is risky (6.4%) than not risky (0.5%); they are more likely to say a hazardous situation or substance is present (11.0%) than not present (0.9%). The ratio of alarming to reassuring statements on both risk and presence is considerably more lopsided for unattributed paragraphs than for the average of all sources. This suggests that reporters' summaries of the risk situation are less balanced (more alarming) than the evidence they cite from sources.

Mixed. Paragraphs that cited more than one source ("mixed") asserted risk more than any other source in the archive (56.8%). Mixed paragraphs also denied risk and took an intermediate position on risk more than the overall averages, but by much smaller margins.

While mixed paragraphs account for a relatively small number of paragraphs in the archive (3.5%), they figure rather more prominently on the article level (27.0%). A representative paragraph from a mixed source might read: "Federal, state, and local officials agreed with citizens and workers at last night's meeting that the situation was dangerous." This type of paragraph is relatively common in the articles, especially those about landfills.

The subject of presence was discussed infrequently in mixed attribution paragraphs. No–risk–information paragraphs were lowest in this category (24.2%). By far the most common mixed source paragraph, in other words, is a paragraph that asserts risk.

Other. Paragraphs that did not fall into any of the above categories ("other") were predominantly about subjects other than risk. Of the sixteen "other" paragraphs, 87.5% had no risk information and 12.5% (two paragraphs) asserted the presence of a hazard.

Table 2.6 summarizes the relationships between source and risk in the archive. The six indented categories are the first six columns from Table 2.5—that is, the six kinds of risk approach other than no risk information. To this, four composite measures have been added: (1) "Attention to Risk" is the sum of "Assert Risk," "Deny Risk," and "Middle (on risk)"—it thus represents the percentage of all paragraphs citing a particular source that deal with risk; (2) "Alarm Ratio" is "Assert Risk" divided by "Deny Risk"—it thus represents the preponderance of risk assertions over risk denials for the particular source (an Alarm Ratio of 1.0 indicates equal numbers of risk–asserting and risk–denying paragraphs; (3) "Certainty Ratio" is "Assert Risk" plus "Deny Risk," the sum divided by "Middle (on risk)"—it thus represents the extent to which a particular source tends to take firm or extreme positions rather than middling ones (a source with equal numbers of paragraphs in each of the three categories would have a Certainty Ratio of 2.0); (4) "Attention to Presence" is the sum of "Assert Presence," "Deny Presence," and "Middle (on presence)"—it thus represents the percentage of all paragraphs citing a particular source that deal with presence. In the columns "Sources with High Averages" and "Sources with Low Averages," Table 2.6 lists the sources which are on either extreme in the categories of risk described above and compares them with the overall average for all sources. Table 2.6 also lists sources with averages near the overall average.

In summary, then, the sources that pay most attention to risk are mixed sources, workers, experts, and citizens. The sources that pay least attention

TABLE 2.6
Summary of Source–Risk Relationships

Category of Risk	Overall Average	Sources with High Averages		Sources with Intermediate Averages		Sources with Low Averages	
Attention to Risk	17.4%	Mixed 68.2%	Experts 33.9%	State 17.7%	Advocacy 19.9%	County 8.6%	Industry 12.5%
		Workers 36.3	Citizens 27.4	Local 18.6	Govt Gen 21.3	Unattrib. 9.7	Federal 16.2
Assert Risk	10.0	Mixed 56.8	Citizens 16.3	Local 7.9	State 10.2	Industry 1.6	County 6.4
		Experts 21.2	Workers 15.1	Govt Gen 8.6	Advocacy 13.4	Unattrib. 6.4	Federal 7.1
Deny Risk	3.2	Workers 9.1	Experts 6.9	Citizens 3.6	Federal 5.4	Advocacy 0.4	County 0.6
		Industry 8.2	Govt Gen 6.9	Mixed 4.8	Local 6.3	Unattrib. 0.5	State 1.9
Middle on Risk	4.2	Workers 12.1	Mixed 6.6	Local 4.4	Govt Gen 5.8	County 1.6	Unattrib. 2.8
		Citizens 7.5	Advocacy 6.1	State 5.6	Experts 5.8	Industry 2.7	Federal 3.7
Attention to Presence	15.0	Workers 22.2	Experts 20.0	Unattrib. 13.4	State 17.1	Mixed 7.5	Local 11.9
		Federal 20.8	Citizens 19.2	Advocacy 13.7	Industry 18.3	Govt Gen 10.9	County 12.9
Assert Presence	10.2	Workers 22.2	Citizens 12.4	Industry 8.6	Advocacy 11.2	Mixed 4.0	Govt Gen 7.8
		Federal 12.8	Experts 11.7	Unattrib. 11.0	State 11.5	Local 5.2	County 8.1
Deny Presence	2.3	Industry 7.5	Federal 3.0	State 1.8	Mixed 2.2	Workers 0.0	County 1.3
		Experts 4.7	Local 2.9	Advocacy 1.8	Citizens 2.6	Unattrib. 0.9	Govt Gen 1.7
Middle on Presence	2.5	Federal 5.0	State 3.8	Unattrib. 1.5	County 3.5	Workers 0.0	Mixed 1.3
		Citizens 4.2	Local 3.8	Industry 2.2	Experts 3.6	Advocacy 0.7	Govt Gen 1.4

Category of Risk	Overall Ratio	Sources with High Ratios		Sources with Intermediate Ratios		Sources with Low Ratios	
Alarm Ratio: (Assert Risk/Deny Risk)	3.1	Advocacy 33.5	Mixed 11.8	Workers 1.7	Citizens 4.5	Industry 0.2	Local 1.3
		Unattrib. 12.8	County 10.7	Experts 3.1	State 5.4	Govt Gen 1.2	Federal 1.3
Certainty Ratio: ((Assert Risk + Deny Risk)/Middle on Risk)	3.1	Mixed 9.3	County 4.4	Govt Gen 2.7	Local 3.2	Workers 2.0	Advocacy 2.3
		Experts 4.8	Industry 3.6	Citizens 2.7	Federal 3.4	State 2.2	Unattrib. 2.5

are county government, unattributed sources, industry, and federal government.

The sources most likely to assert risk are mixed sources, experts, citizens, and workers. Least likely to assert risk are industry, county government, unattributed sources, and federal government.

Workers, industry, experts, and government general are most likely to deny risk, while advocacy groups, unattributed sources, county government, and state government are least likely to deny risk.

Middling opinions about risk are most likely to come from workers, citizens, mixed sources, and advocacy groups. The sources least likely to give middling opinions on risk are county government, industry, unattributed sources, and federal government.

Sources high on the alarm ratio—that is, sources having a preponderance of risk–asserting paragraphs over risk–denying paragraphs—are advocacy groups, unattributed sources, mixed sources, and county government. Sources with a low alarm ratio are industry, government general, and local and federal government.

Sources that tend to be cited on extreme rather than middling positions—that is, those high on the certainty ratio—are mixed sources, experts, county government, and industry. Low on the certainty ratio are workers, state government, advocacy groups, and unattributed sources.

On the subject of presence, the sources that pay most attention to presence are workers, federal government, experts, and citizens. Sources that pay least attention to presence are mixed sources, government general, and local and county government.

Sources that have high averages for asserting presence are workers, federal government, citizens, and experts. Mixed sources, local government, government general, and county government have low averages for asserting presence.

Sources most likely to deny presence are industry, experts, and federal and local government. Least likely to deny presence are workers, unattributed sources, county government, and government general.

Finally, sources that are most likely to be in the middle about presence are federal government, citizens, and state and local government. Sources least likely to be in the middle on presence are workers, advocacy groups, mixed sources, and government general.

WHERE DOES EACH RISK STATEMENT COME FROM? Another useful way to examine the source–risk relationship in the archive is to look at paragraphs that take different approaches to risk—risky, not risky, present, not present, and so on—and see which source they come from. Table 2.7 shows the percentage of each risk that is attributable to each source; unlike Table 2.5, in Table 2.7 the *vertical columns* sum to 100.0%.

TABLE 2.7
Percentage of Paragraphs of Each Risk Approach to Each Source
(vertical columns sum to 100%)

Source	Risky (%)	Not Risky (%)	Mixed Opinion (if Risky) (%)	Risky Substance Present (%)	Risky Substance not Present (%)	Mixed Opinion (if present) (%)	No Risk Info. (%)	Average for All Risk Approaches (%)
Federal Government	3.2	7.8	4.0	5.7	6.0	9.3	4.3	4.6
State Government	14.9	8.7	19.3	16.7	11.4	22.4	14.2	14.7
County Government	3.1	1.0	1.8	3.8	2.7	6.8	5.5	4.8
Local Government	5.8	14.6	7.7	3.8	9.4	11.2	7.6	7.4
Government General	4.8	12.1	7.7	4.2	4.0	3.1	5.6	5.5
Industry	1.5	25.2	6.2	8.3	32.2	8.7	10.0	9.8
Workers	2.3	4.4	4.4	3.3	0.0	0.0	0.9	1.5
Advocacy Groups	5.7	0.5	6.2	4.7	3.4	1.2	4.2	4.3
Citizens	7.7	5.3	8.4	5.7	5.4	8.1	3.7	4.7
Experts	8.9	9.2	5.8	4.8	8.7	6.2	2.9	4.2
Unattributed	22.1	5.8	23.0	37.3	13.4	21.1	39.5	34.7
Mixed	19.8	5.3	5.5	1.4	3.4	1.9	1.2	3.5
Other	0.0	0.0	0.0	0.3	0.0	0.0	0.3	0.2

Risk assertions. When paragraphs assert that a situation is risky, as they do in 10% of the archive, the information is coming from unattributed sources (22.1%), mixed sources (19.8%), and the state government (14.9%). Experts contribute 8.9% of the paragraphs that say a situation is risky, which is more than twice the overall percentage of paragraphs attributed to experts in the archive. On the other hand, industry contributes only 1.5% of the paragraphs that assert risk, the lowest of any source except "other," which contributes none. The federal government is also low, contributing only 3.2% of the risky paragraphs.

Risk denials. Industry is by far the leading source for risk–denying information. Over 25% of the paragraphs that claim a situation is not risky come from industry, as opposed to the next highest sources—local government (14.6%), general government (12.1%), and experts (9.2%). Advocacy groups and county government are rarely the source of risk–denying paragraphs (0.5% and 1.0% respectively).

Mixed risk. Of the paragraphs that present a mixed opinion on whether a situation is risky, 23.0% are unattributed and 19.3% come from the state government. The county government is rarely the source for mixed opinions on risk (1.8%).

Presence assertions. When paragraphs say a hazardous situation is present, they come most often from unattributed sources (37.3%). The next highest source is the state government (16.7%). County and local governments (3.8%), workers (3.3%), and mixed sources (1.4%) assert presence the least frequently of all sources.

Presence denials. Statements that risk is not present come primarily from industry; 32.2% of the time the archive contains a denial that a hazard is present, the source of the denial is industry. Other high sources of denials are unattributed sources (13.4%) and the state government (11.4%), with local government (9.4%) and experts (8.7%) also fairly high. Workers never deny the presence of a hazard, while county government (2.7%), advocacy groups (3.4%), and mixed sources (3.4%) are small contributors to presence–denying paragraphs in the archive.

Mixed presence. The state government (22.4%) and unattributed sources (21.1%) are the most usual sources for mixed opinions on presence. Local government contributes 11.2% of the mixed opinions on presence, and the federal government is the source in 9.3% of the paragraphs that have mixed opinions on presence. Advocacy groups are rarely the source of mixed opinions on presence (1.2%); workers never are. Mixed sources (1.9%) and general government (3.1%) are also low.

No risk information. Of the paragraphs that do not discuss risk at all, 39.5% come from unattributed sources, 14.2% from state government, and

10.0% from industry. Workers (0.9%), mixed sources (1.2%), and experts (2.9%) supply very little of the information that does not deal with risk.

Relationship between Article Position and Source

This analysis centers on where particular sources are likely to be placed in an article—that is, the tendency of newspapers to cite certain sources in the first five or ten paragraphs of an article, while other sources are cited later (for a smaller readership, of course). Table 2.8 shows the relative frequency of each source in the first five, second five, and first ten paragraphs of each article in the archive, as opposed to the overall frequency of that source.

Not surprisingly, there is a large tendency for unattributed paragraphs to occur early in the article. The basic who, what, where, when, why, and how information that generally leads off an article seldom requires attribution. Of the first five paragraphs in the articles, 50.3% were unattributed, versus 34.7% overall. It is noteworthy, however, that in the analysis of source and risk in the previous section, unattributed sources were also responsible for much of the information about risk, especially risk assertions. Such unattributed risk assertions may be leading off many articles.

All other sources are less prominent in the first five paragraphs than at a later point in the article. State government, for example, comprised 11.3%

TABLE 2.8
Position of Sources in the First 10 Paragraphs

Source	1st 5		2nd 5		1st 10		Overall	
	# of Par.	% of Par.	# of Par.	% of Par.	# of Par.	% of Par.	# of Par.	% of Par.
Federal Government	56	4.5	69	5.8	125	5.1	297	4.6
State Government	140	11.3	202	16.9	342	14.0	954	14.7
County Government	51	4.1	59	4.9	110	4.5	310	4.8
Local Government	72	5.8	112	9.4	184	7.6	479	7.4
Government General	63	5.1	93	7.8	156	6.4	360	5.6
Industry	68	5.5	81	6.8	149	6.1	636	9.8
Workers	11	0.9	13	1.1	24	1.0	99	1.5
Advocacy Groups	34	2.7	38	3.2	72	3.0	277	4.3
Citizens	43	3.5	45	3.8	88	3.6	306	4.7
Experts	44	3.5	41	3.4	85	3.5	274	4.2
Unattributed	624	50.3	423	35.6	1047	43.0	2251	34.7
Mixed	31	2.5	17	1.4	48	2.0	227	3.5
Other	3	0.2	2	0.2	5	0.2	16	0.2
Total	1240		1195		2435		6486	

of the first five paragraphs versus 14.7% overall; it was still the most frequent attribution in the early paragraphs, with local government (5.8%)
next.

In the second five paragraphs, unattributed sources (35.6%) yield to the
government (44.8% combined, versus 30.8% in the first five paragraphs and
37.1% overall). All five government sources score higher in the second five
paragraphs than overall, while all five non–government sources score
higher overall than in the second five paragraphs. Basically, the scenario of
this analysis reflects a "typical" news story: the first five paragraphs tell
what happened (without much attribution, though in some cases the state
government gets in an early quote); then, after the basic facts, the article
turns to the most credible available authority, government, for con-
firmation and elaboration. Other sources—industry, workers, advocacy
groups, citizens, and experts—come later.

Relationship between Article Position and Risk Approach

The same question can be asked of article position and risk category: do
newspapers tend to adopt one risk approach early in the article and another later on? Table 2.9 shows the frequency of risk approaches in the first
five, the second five, and the first ten paragraphs, as opposed to their
frequency overall.

The differences are very small. There seems to be a tendency for risk-
asserting and presence–asserting paragraphs to come early, and for risk-
denying and presence–denying paragraphs to come later. But what is most
striking about these data is the small size of the differences. Critics often
assert that news headlines and leads tend to be more alarming than the rest
of the article—a claim made in the subjective expert assessment of this
archive as well. Headlines were not coded—but there is little evidence in
the content analysis of sensational leads.

Relationship between Article Type and Source

Table 2.10 shows the results of an analysis of type of news article—hard
news, feature, background, and investigative—as it relates to source.
Sources do vary, it would seem, depending on the type of news. Local and
county governments, and to a lesser extent state governments were considerably more likely to be sources for hard news stories than for other types
of stories. This is not surprising, since these levels of government are generally the ones on the scene of a breaking environmental story. Citizens and
mixed sources were also used more in hard news than in softer news.
Unattributed paragraphs, on the other hand, were less common in hard

TABLE 2.9
Position of Risk Categories in the First 10 Paragraphs

Risk Category	1st 5		2nd 5		1st 10		Overall	
	# of Par.	% of Par.	# of Par.	% of Par.	# of Par.	% of Par.	# of Par.	% of Par.
Risky	125	10.1	111	9.3	236	9.7	650	10.0
Not Risky	32	2.6	35	2.9	67	2.8	206	3.2
Mixed Opinion (if risky)	44	3.5	61	5.1	105	4.3	274	4.2
Risky Substance Present	170	13.7	134	11.2	304	12.5	662	10.2
Risky Substance Not Present	23	1.6	23	1.9	46	1.9	149	2.3
Mixed Opinion (if present)	36	2.9	36	3.0	72	3.0	161	2.5
No Risk Information	810	65.3	795	66.5	1605	65.9	4384	67.6
Total	1240		1195		2435		6486	

TABLE 2.10
Relationship between Article Type and Source
(analysis on the paragraph level)

Source	Overall % (n = 6486)	Hard News % (n = 2592)	Feature % (n = 2407)	Background % (n = 719)	Investigative % (n = 745)
Federal Government	4.6	3.2	7.1	5.3	0.7
State Government	14.7	18.6	11.0	9.5	18.5
County Government	4.8	9.7	2.2	0.6	0.4
Local Government	7.4	12.4	4.1	5.4	2.4
Government General	5.5	4.0	9.1	3.6	1.3
Industry	9.8	7.8	8.0	11.3	21.3
Workers	1.5	0.9	1.3	0.0	5.9
Advocacy Groups	4.3	3.8	6.1	3.6	0.7
Citizens	4.7	5.3	6.4	1.4	0.7
Experts	4.2	3.4	4.2	9.0	2.8
Unattributed	34.7	25.0	38.8	49.0	39.9
Mixed	3.5	5.9	1.4	1.2	4.2
Other	0.2	0.1	0.2	0.1	1.2

news than elsewhere; this was also true of the federal government and most non–government sources.

For feature stories, the federal government, general government, and especially citizens and advocacy groups were more likely to be cited. The number of unattributed sources also increased, while local, county, and state government were cited less frequently than in other article types.

In articles that supplied background material, unattributed sources, industry, and experts were more heavily relied on than in other article types. Federal government was also cited more than the overall average. Reliance on the other four levels of government, especially county government, was lower than average for background stories. Attention to workers, citizens, and advocacy groups was also scanty in background stories.

For investigative reporting, industry, state government, workers, and unattributed and mixed sources were the primary sources of information, as one would expect of stories that generally look into industry practices and state efforts to control them. Investigative stories relied less on local, county, and federal government, and contributions by citizen and advocacy groups were insignificant.

Overall, then, hard news stories rely heavily on those who are on the scene—that is, local, county, and state government; features "feature" largely citizens and advocacy groups; industry, experts, and unattributed sources provide background material; and industry and workers are important sources in investigative pieces, along with state government.

Relationship between Article Type and Risk Approach

Table 2.11 shows the relationship between the type of news story and the risk approach. The differences are small but provocative.

Hard news stories contain more risk–asserting paragraphs than the overall average for all article types, and fewer risk–denying and mixed paragraphs. But for presence the opposite pattern prevails: presence assertions are less common than in all the other article types, while presence denials and mixed paragraphs are more common.

Features are a mirror image of hard news. Paragraphs on risk tend toward the reassuring and mixed side more than in other article types, while paragraphs on presence tend toward the alarming side.

Background articles have fewer no–risk–information paragraphs and more paragraphs dealing with risk; risk–affirming paragraphs are more common than in other article types, but so are risk–denying and mixed paragraphs. Background articles, in other words, tend to say more about risk.

Investigative articles, on the other hand, tend to say more about pres-

TABLE 2.11
Relationship between Article Type and Risk Category
(analysis on the paragraph level)

Risk Category	Overall % (n = 6486)	Hard News % (n = 2592)	Feature % (n = 2407)	Background % (n = 719)	Investigative % (n = 745)
Risky	10.0	10.8	8.3	12.8	9.8
Not Risky	3.2	2.5	4.3	3.9	1.3
Mixed Opinion (if risky)	4.2	3.7	5.2	6.0	1.1
Risky Substance Present	10.2	8.8	10.4	9.9	14.9
Risky Substance Not Present	2.3	2.7	2.0	2.6	1.6
Mixed Opinion (if present)	2.5	3.3	1.9	1.5	2.7
No Risk Information	67.6	68.3	67.8	63.3	68.6

ence. They also tend to be more alarming, with relatively few risk–denying, presence–denying, and mixed paragraphs compared to the more frequent risk–asserting and presence–asserting paragraphs.

Relationships within Source Categories

The inclusion of one particular source in an article sometimes has a systematic relationship with the inclusion of another source. For example, an article that cites the federal government could be more likely or less likely than an article without federal sources to cite the state government as well, or the two sources could have no relationship. To test for these source–source relationships, two–way cross–tabulations were calculated for every possible combination of sources. Table 2.12 shows the relationships (positive or negative) that were statistically significant at p < .05 or better.

Thus, for example, the table shows that articles citing industry tend to cite state government as well, a relationship large enough that it would occur by chance less than five times in a hundred. By contrast, articles that cite industry are *less* likely to cite county government as well. There is no statistically significant relationship between whether an article cites industry and whether it cites the federal government.

The seventeen significant findings from this analysis do not form an easily interpreted pattern, but they do reveal some unexpected characteristics of the archive:

- Articles that cite the federal government are more likely to cite county government, advocacy groups, and experts.
- Articles that cite the state government are more likely to cite county government, industry, experts, and mixed sources.
- Articles that cite county government are more likely to cite the federal government, state government, and local government; they are less likely to cite industry.
- Articles that cite local government are more likely to cite county government and citizens; they are less likely to cite industry.
- Articles that cite general government are less likely to cite advocacy groups.
- Articles that cite industry are more likely to cite state government, experts, and mixed sources; they are less likely to cite county government, local government, and citizens.
- Articles that cite advocacy groups are more likely to cite federal government and mixed sources; they are less likely to cite general government.
- Articles that cite citizens are more likely to cite local government; they are less likely to cite industry.

TABLE 2.12
Relationships within Source Categories

	Fed. Gov't.	State Gov't.	County Gov't.	Local Gov't.	Gov't. Gen.	Industry	Workers	Advocacy Groups	Citizens	Experts	Unattrib.	Mixed	Other
Federal Government	X												
State Government	–	X											
County Government	Pos*	Pos**	X										
Local Government	–	–	Pos*	X									
Government General	–	–	–	–	X								
Industry	–	Pos*	Neg**	Neg*	–	X							
Workers	–	–	–	–	–	–	X						
Advocacy Groups	Pos*	–	–	–	Neg**	–	–	X					
Citizens	–	–	–	Pos**	–	Neg**	–	–	X				
Experts	Pos**	Pos**	–	–	–	Pos*	–	–	–	X			
Unattributed	–	–	–	–	–	–	–	–	–	–	X		
Mixed	–	Pos**	–	–	–	Pos**	–	Pos**	–	Pos**	–	X	
Other	–	–	–	–	–	–	–	–	–	–	–	–	X

* p < .05
** p < .01

- Articles that cite experts are more likely to cite federal government, state government, industry, and mixed sources.
- Articles that cite mixed sources are more likely to cite state government, industry, advocacy groups, and experts.

Of the seventeen relationships significant at p < .05 or better, six involved industry (three positive and three negative). This indicates that an article's use or non-use of industry sources is systematically related to its use or non-use of other sources. State government, county government, experts, and mixed sources showed four significant relationships each. By contrast, there were no significant relationships for workers.

Relationships within Risk Categories

Two-way cross-tabulations were calculated for the six risk categories (not counting the no-risk-information category) to determine the relationship between the presence or absence of a particular risk approach in an article and the presence or absence of each of the other risk approaches in that article. Table 2.13 presents the results. All were positive, and ten out of fifteen possible relationships were statistically significant at p < .05 or better. In other words, articles that treat risk at all tend to treat it in several ways.

The patterns here are easy to interpret. On the subject of presence, for example, presence-asserting, presence-denying, and mixed paragraphs were all interrelated positively; that is, articles that deal with presence in any of the three ways show a strong tendency to deal with it in all three ways. Similarly, the risk-asserting, risk-denying, and mixed-risk categories were also positively interrelated, suggesting that one risk approach tends to be accompanied by the others.

Not surprisingly, there were strong relationships also between risk-as-

TABLE 2.13
Relationships within Risk Categories

	Risky	Not Risky	Mixed (if Risky)	Present	Not Present	Mixed (if present)
Risky	X					
Not Risky	Pos*	X				
Mixed (if risky)	Pos**	Pos*	X			
Present	Pos**	–	Pos*	X		
Not Present	Pos*	Pos**	–	Pos**	X	
Mixed (if present)	–	–	–	Pos**	Pos**	X

* p < .05
** p < .01

serting and presence–asserting paragraphs and between risk–denying and presence–denying paragraphs.

These interrelationships do not of course mean equal attention to the six risk categories. As we have seen, the archive includes many more risk–asserting than risk–denying or mixed paragraphs, and many more presence–asserting than presence–denying or mixed paragraphs. Nonetheless, it is an important finding that paragraphs with different risk approaches tend to be found in the same articles rather than in different ones. A typical environmental risk article, in short, includes more alarming than reassuring paragraphs, but it does tend to include *some* paragraphs of both sorts.

To explore these interrelationships further, a "risk window" was constructed extending two paragraphs on each side of a particular paragraph. This question was then asked: What is the distribution of risk approaches immediately surrounding paragraphs of each risk approach? For example, how often is a risk–denying paragraph found within two paragraphs on either side of a risk–claiming paragraph? Table 2.14 presents these results.

For every risk approach, the most common paragraph to find nearby was no–risk–information. This is not surprising, since two–thirds of all paragraphs in the archive were non–risk. However, no–risk–information paragraphs were less common near risk–related paragraphs than near each other, indicating a tendency for paragraphs about risk to cluster near each other.

No–risk–information paragraphs aside, risk–asserting paragraphs were most frequently near other risk–asserting paragraphs (26.0%) or near presence–asserting paragraphs (15.7%). Only 5.3% of the paragraphs near risk–asserting paragraphs denied the risk, and only 8.0% expressed a mixed view. Most risk assertions, in other words, were not balanced nearby.

Risk–denying paragraphs, on the other hand, were accompanied by risk–asserting paragraphs nearly as often as by other risk–denying paragraphs (15.0% versus 15.9%). Mixed paragraphs on risk were also fairly common (9.7%), while risk–denying paragraphs only occasionally were near paragraphs about presence. Thus risk denials in the archive, less frequent than risk assertions, were balanced nearby far more often when they occurred.

Mixed paragraphs on risk were near risk–asserting paragraphs more often than they were near other mixed paragraphs (16.8% versus 12.3%). Although risk–denying paragraphs appeared near mixed ones twice as often as they appeared overall (7.1% versus 3.2%), the typical mixed paragraph on risk is still near paragraphs asserting risk and asserting presence (10.1%). When a mixed risk paragraph is found, in other words, it tends to be the most reassuring paragraph around, balancing a risk assertion rather than a risk denial.

TABLE 2.14
Relationships within Risk Categories
("risk windows")

Risk Category	Risky %	Not Risky %	Mixed Opinion (if Risky) %	Risky Sub. Present %	Risky Sub. Not Present %	Mixed Opinion (if present) %	No Risk Info. %
Risky	26.0	5.3	8.0	15.7	1.2	1.8	42.0
Not Risky	15.0	15.9	9.7	4.1	3.9	1.1	50.3
Mixed Opinion (if risky)	16.8	7.1	12.3	10.1	2.4	1.4	49.8
Risky Substance Present	14.9	1.4	4.6	19.1	3.2	5.3	51.6
Risky Substance Not Present	4.7	5.4	4.7	13.4	14.9	6.8	50.2
Mixed Opinion (if present)	6.2	1.4	2.4	19.6	6.0	10.0	54.5
No Risk Information	8.2	3.5	4.7	10.6	2.5	3.0	67.6
Overall Average	10.0	3.2	4.2	10.2	2.3	2.5	67.6

The pattern for presence is virtually identical. Presence–asserting paragraphs are accompanied mostly by other presence–asserting paragraphs and by paragraphs asserting risk; they are seldom balanced by nearby denials. Presence-denying paragraphs are accompanied by presence-asserting paragraphs nearly as often as by other denials; they are much more often balanced nearby. Mixed presence paragraphs are accompanied by presence assertions more often than by presence denials, though both are more common near the mixed paragraphs than in the overall archive.

In sum, the various risk approaches are all positively interrelated—more likely to appear in the same articles than in different ones. But because alarming paragraphs are much more common than reassuring ones, a reassuring paragraph is very likely to be balanced by a nearby alarming one, while many alarming paragraphs are not accompanied by any nearby reassurance.

The foregoing analysis has focused almost exclusively on two characteristics of the environmental risk archive—source and risk approach. It has yielded considerable information about the content of the most highly professional journalism about environmental risk. But much that is worth knowing about environmental risk reporting—tone, objectivity, completeness, etc.—is difficult to quantify in a formal content analysis. For insight into these matters, we turn now to the expert analysis of the archive.

3

Expert Analysis of the Environmental Risk Archive

To complement and extend the formal content analysis with a richer subjective analysis, four experts—a journalist, an environmental activist, an industry representative, and a scientist—were asked to spend an intensive weekend reading and analyzing various aspects of the archive, including treatment of risk, tone, bias, accuracy, clarity, enterprise, newsworthiness, and individual differences.

Methods

The experts selected to review the archive were chosen for their different points of view as well as their outstanding professional reputations. The four experts were:

- Jim Detjen, environmental reporter, *Philadelphia Inquirer.*
- James Lanard, legislative agent, New Jersey Environmental Lobby.
- Eugene Murphy, Manager, Public Information, Public Service Electric and Gas Company of New Jersey.
- James Sederis, environmental consultant, A.J. Sederis Consultants.

For the purpose of later discussion, the experts will be referred to by their respective stereotypes: journalist, activist, industry representative, and scientist.

Over the weekend of August 23–25, 1985, the four experts met with investigators of the Environmental Risk Reporting Project for an intensive weekend of archive review, evaluation, and discussion. Each person was given a packet that consisted of the archive divided into six parts to allow for alternating periods of reading and discussion. (A schedule of reading/discussion times and instructions are in Appendix B.) The experts were instructed to read, or at least skim, every article for overall strengths and weaknesses, good examples and bad examples. (A caution was given here for the judges to differentiate between a serious problem likely to affect the reader's understanding of environmental risk and a professional quibble.)

The experts were asked to take notes as they read, commenting on those articles that triggered comments. In order to organize thinking and note-taking and facilitate discussions about the articles, the project coordinators had prepared a list of proposed standards against which the articles could be judged. They are as follows:

1. *Treatment of risk assessment variables*—Does the article deal appropriately with the degree of risk represented by the situation it discusses? Does it have enough information on risk assessment, as opposed to other aspects of the story? If there are risk comparisons, are they appropriately and accurately used? Are health probabilities and other aspects of risk assessment properly used?

2. *Tone*—Does the article find the right balance of calmness and concern, or is the tone too sensational, too reassuring, too outraged, too resigned, too neutral? Do headlines or lead paragraphs create a different impression than the rest of the article justifies? Is language used in ways that might distort the reader's impressions? Are photos and other graphics appropriately used? Is the story overplayed or underplayed? Is the mix of opinions and information, and of extreme opinions and moderate opinions, appropriate? Does the article tend to involve, or terrorize, or pacify, or alienate the lay reader?

3. *Objectivity/fairness/balance/bias*—Does the article seem to lean in a particular direction? Does the reporter seem emotionally involved in the story? Is the reporter making judgments, directly or indirectly? Has the reporter relied on appropriate sources, as opposed to biased or unreliable ones? Are certain sources or points of view underrepresented?

4. *Accuracy/completeness/thoroughness/factuality*—Is anything wrong or missing in the article, or is it complete and error-free? Does the article use technical information appropriately and correctly? Does the article correctly handle technical vocabulary, theory, and methodology? Does it draw conclusions that are not justified by the information presented?

5. *Clarity/understandability/interest/writing quality*—Does the article do an especially good or an especially poor job of making the information accessible to readers? Are the facts presented in an understandable way, so that a layperson can figure out what happened and why it matters? Is the writing effective?

6. *Enterprise*—Is there too much or too little investigative digging? Are reporters "going after" stories or covering what happens? Are they finding their own sources or relying on public relations and sources at the scene? Are they discovering issues before they break or on their own? Are they exploring relevant background once the story breaks?

7. *Newsworthiness*—Have the editors chosen the best articles? Are these the big issues of environmental risk, the right topics to be writing about? What is here that should not be, and what is not here that should be?
8. *Resources/geography/individual differences*—Do particular newspapers seem to be doing a particularly good or exceptionally poor job? Particular reporters? What differences do you find between the work of big newspapers and smaller ones? What differences do you find between the work of North Jersey and South Jersey newspapers? Are there topics which seem to provoke especially good or especially poor reporting?

A separate page was provided for notes on each standard. Thus, if a particular article triggered a comment about bias, for example, the expert would write the comment and the identification number of the article on the notes page dealing with objectivity and bias. Experts were also encouraged to make any other comments that seemed useful.

In addition to the separate notes pages, the four experts wrote overall summaries of their impressions of the articles at the end of the weekend. All discussions were tape recorded; the following results are based on the taped discussions, the notes the experts took while reading the archive, and the experts' overall evaluations of the articles' strengths and weaknesses.

Results

Treatment of Risk Assessment Variables

One judgment that all four experts overwhelmingly agreed on was that information on environmental risk is scanty even in articles selected as the best examples of environmental risk reporting. In overall summaries where the experts were asked to write about their general impressions of the archive as a whole, the insufficiency of environmental risk information was cited most frequently:

> Overall, I have found very little environmental risk reporting in the hundreds of articles we looked at. With a few exceptions. . . most reporters simply don't discuss risk.
>
> *Journalist*
>
> As a group, we seemed to feel that the treatment of risk left a great deal to be desired. The risk created by an environmental incident to human health and/ or the environment is what it's all about. How the risk is coped with, controlled, or eliminated makes the news.
>
> *Scientist*
>
> There was a woeful lack, in almost all cases, of an effort to measure what the hazard meant—the risk assessment question. . . .
>
> *Industry representative*

Surprisingly, there was very little meaningful environmental risk reporting in the archive. I had expected to read a good deal about the risks associated. . . with a leak or a spill. As it turns out, I didn't read very much about risk.

Activist

The panel agreed that the articles from which risk news was most conspicuously absent were the hard news items. Series, features, and "think pieces" that were longer and better researched tended to cover risk more completely than breaking stories did.

The panel frequently gave reporters the blame for the articles' lack of information. Lack of industry, ignorance of the subject, deadline pressures, and the complexity of the issues caused reporters to neglect risk or to report it incompletely, according to the panel. A *Herald News* article about the siting of a garbage incineration plant, for example, mentions that an opponent of the incinerator "contends the plant will emit dioxin, a suspected carcinogen."[1] The article focuses instead, however, largely on the truck traffic generated by the project and does not discuss further the risk of dioxin exposure.

The panel's reaction to this article included speculation that the reporter did not know how to get the pertinent information, that the article was not carefully written, and that the reporter mentioned the risk almost as an afterthought. The journalist on the panel cited the "inexperience on the part of reporters . . . general assignment reporters don't know the questions to ask, . . . don't know how to insert information into the story."

Another reason reporters leave out information on risk, according to the panel, was the assumption that readers already know about it. "Risk is so casually mentioned in the articles that it's like people have read five stories in depth [on the topic]. . . . They don't want to bore the readers presenting background," stated the activist. "What I decided must be going on is that the reporters have made assumptions that the reader knows what the . . . risks are."

All experts on the panel agreed that environmental risk is a difficult subject to report on and that in many cases the information is scarce or complicated. However, they believed that there was more to the lack of reporting than that. Reporters do not seem to be able to put an incident into its environmental context, the panel felt; they do not know what the environmental issues are and, in some cases, do not seem to want to know. Many environmental stories are reported by general or municipal reporters, and these reporters simply do not have the background, nor do they make the effort, to report the risk factors in articles.

Moreover, reporters seem much more interested in covering the political issues that inevitably surround such environmental questions as landfill siting. The journalist commented: "Most of the landfill stories we've been sent, I think 90% of them are dealing with the political issues. Only 10% or less even delve into the leachate problems or some of the environmental or risk problems."

In general, the panel felt that environmental politics make up the "everyday meat and potatoes of a general assignment reporter" that the reporter feels very comfortable covering; he or she must work much harder to uncover the risk aspect of an environmental situation.

The panel found that in many stories the impact of an environmental situation on the individual is rarely discussed—even in stories that are clearly about a threat to human health. In a *News Tribune* story about brown water, for example, nearly every possible aspect of the problem was discussed in detail in the four–part article except the risk to the public's health.[2] On this story the industry representative commented: "They did a great job of covering a lot of aspects of the story and then casually reported somewhere that the iron content was three times the allowable limit. . . . Nobody said, 'well, what does this mean, am I going to rust inside?'"

Even those reporters who are covering environmental stories fairly completely, the panel agreed, will often leave out discussions of risk and will not define the jargon they use when they do report it. The journalist on the panel found that reporters "do not explain basic terms. . . . I'll see people describe priority pollutants. . . . Maybe they've been covering this issue for many months but they should at least explain to the reader in a simple sentence [what priority pollutants are]. . . . There's a lot of jargon that creeps into these kinds of stories. . . ."

Although the reporter writes the story, the final sign–off on a story is the editor's responsibility, and the panel found editors ultimately accountable for the lack of risk information in environmental articles. In the words of the industry representative, "reporters might be inept, but editors are abject." In article after article members of the panel declared that an editor should see the holes in a story even if a reporter cannot. In an ambitious series on waste oil, risk was not mentioned until the last day of the series.[3] Panel members agreed that although the reporter was perhaps too immersed in investigative reporting to put it all in perspective, the editor should have been able to do it. The journalist stated that the series was a "classic case of a reporter getting lost in the trees . . . immersed in the details. . . . There should have been a good editor." Others on the panel also felt that the article suffered from lack of editing, that, in the words of the industry representative, the reporter very often simply "wants to go out and find the crime, and doesn't really assess what the enormity of that might be."

Editors may be cutting risk information out of stories because they feel it is not exciting enough to attract readers, the panel felt. According to the activist, "There are no dead bodies, it's not sexy, and it could be that they [reporters] write it and the editors take it out, because that's the least attractive part of the article."

Tone

Misleading headlines frequently set an inappropriate tone for articles on environmental risk, the panel found. In many cases, headlines were understated or overstated, or completely misrepresented the text of the article. For example, one headline reads "Self–regulation Insufficient for Controlling Spills."[4] The panel found, however, that the text of the article "didn't mesh with the story at all" (activist), and that it was "too strong a statement and probably inaccurate" (journalist).

In other cases, the headline was too sensational for the information in the article and created a feeling of impending doom. "Dioxin Fears Haunt Passaic County" heads an article that discusses the sampling of certain local sites for dioxin.[5] Although the article goes on to say that testing at the local pool and other recreational areas would not begin until the following morning, the headline suggests that the outcome of subsequent analyses are a foregone conclusion. The activist on the panel commented, "They don't even know if there's dioxin and they already hooked the pool users, the children, and the parents right in. . . an amazing jump . . . a cheap shot."

Headlines were also used to "suck readers in" by promising an article on an environmental risk situation and instead covering the politics of a particular environmental controversy. The activist said:

> They need to write these issues as either environmental or political, but not have a misleading lead or headline to get into the politics. . . . They're exploiting the environmental issues to cover the politics. . . . They're not environmental stories to a large extent, [but] they're being presented as environmental stories.

Although the panelists agreed that both the political and the risk aspects of environmental issues need to be written about, they felt it was important to make the distinction between the two and not mislead or misinform the readers.

The panel found that colorful language and descriptions often gave articles an anti–industry tone—for example, the use of the word "dumping" instead of "discharging" in this headline, "Chemical Dumping Checked."[6] Unfortunately, the tendency for articles to take on an anti–industry tone when technical terms are translated into their non–technical equivalents seems to be a characteristic of environmental risk reporting. The experts noted that in other fields—genetic engineering, for example—when the article goes from technical to colorful, it sells the technology. While everyone on the panel agreed that "dumping" is more likely to have an emotional impact on the reader, there was some disagreement over whether "decoding" a basically neutral technical term to a more interesting, clear, jargon–free but perhaps more volatile common term (for example, rapid oxidation versus explosion) would necessarily lead to a biased tone. "Too many environmental reporters use too much jargon; 'discharge' is to me, jargon," commented the journalist. "I would rather have someone decode the jargon. You can have good reporting with a slight point of view."

The industry representative and the scientist objected to decoding because it simplifies the issue and causes inaccuracies. "The reporter wants a simple explanation of something, and if there isn't a simple explanation, he gets frustrated," commented the industry representative. "He's dealing, in many ways, from an eleven–year–old angle that says is this going to happen and if it isn't, what's going to happen?"

The panel found that reporters are responsible for the tone of the text but that editors are not reading with sufficient sensitivity to tone. Also, everyone agreed that the editors who write headlines are responsible for the inappropriateness in that area.

Objectivity/Fairness/Balance/Bias

With panelists on both sides of the environmental fence, accusations of bias against one side or the other were expected by both the experts and the project. What the panel found, however, was that although bias existed in the archive, it was on an individual basis that could not be connected with any overall bias for or against a certain group. With few exceptions, the panel agreed that "lazy reporting and editing" contributed to the appearance of bias more than an actual intent by reporters or editors to tip the balance.

The most common examples of bias were stories in which the source of the article—the person or group that brought the story to the reporter's attention—was covered and quoted more extensively than opposing points of view. The activist noted: "There was a trend to not quote industry sources if it was a citizens group that started the news story . . . but we have articles on both sides." In these cases, there was a general feeling that lack of research contributed to the biased result, that the article would have been balanced if the reporter had taken the trouble or had had the time to do some follow–up, or if the editor had caught the bias and insisted on a more balanced treatment of the subject.

In some cases, experts on the panel disagreed on what constituted lazy reporting and what was outright bias. A post–Bhopal article brought this comment from the scientist: "This article is slanted towards completely destroying the public's confidence in the chemical industry. . . . It is filled with implications and untrue statements."[7] The industry person, however, felt the story's bias was due to not enough research, and the activist cited lazy reporting. He said that, particularly where opinions were presented, the reporter had the responsibility to find out more, to produce documentation that supported and/or refuted the opinion so it would not be misconstrued by the reader as fact. All panelists agreed with the statement of the industry representative regarding such "half–done" stories: "I think the public deserves a better shake than that."

A consequence of the tendency of reporters to prefer simple answers rather than to go deeper into the risk issues is an overall dichotomy of risk in the archive; the experts felt that reporters failed to investigate the degrees of risk in an environmental situation. The activist pointed out: "So many of the articles made the assumption that readers will translate the event into danger. . . . They assume that if they report a fire, or an odor, or smoke particulate, that means it's bad. And frankly it is; the question is how bad." The industry representative also felt that the lack of moderateness in the archive was due to the reporters' lack of subtlety in investigating and reporting on risk issues: "General assignment reporters . . . are not aware of what they're dealing with. . . . They're accepting the fact that dioxin is dangerous, that takes care of it, put it in the lead, I don't have to worry about it any more, let's get on with the indictment."

Overall, the experts found the archive to be more alarming than reassuring, but disagreed on whether reality was as bad as the archive says it is. The experts were asked to vote on (1) how alarming they thought reality is relative to the way the archive portrayed it, and (2) how responsible they thought industry is relative to the way the archive portrayed it. The votes were on a ten–point scale, where ten meant "very alarming" or "very irresponsible." For alarm, the scientist, the journalist, and the industry representative felt that the archive was scarier than reality (ten to eight, seven to six, eight to five, respectively). The activist dissented, voting five to seven that the archive did not portray reality as being as frightening as it actually is. On the subject of industry responsibility, the activist again disagreed with the other experts (five to seven, activist; ten to six, scientist; seven to six, journalist; eight to four, industry representative). Basically, the activist felt that even though the archive was alarming, there was not enough risk information in the articles to inform the public about how bad the situation really is: "I've read some of these articles in the past and said 'right on' as an activist. . . . [But] looking at them in a slightly academic manner, I thought, 'So what?' They are catchy and get citizens involved but don't give any content."

The experts were not particularly outraged over the tendency of the archive to be alarming, however. They seemed to think that a reporter's bias in favor of what is alarming is built into the values of journalism and is to be expected. The industry representative pointed out:

> When reporters go out looking for stories, they want news; they don't want to hear how safe the operation is, they don't want to hear about all the safeguards in effect. . . . That's not a news thing . . . that's understandable because their business is to get the news . . . and the specialist reporter or environmental reporter has nothing to do with . . . the essential element of news as news. . . .

Accuracy/Completeness/Thoroughness/Factuality

Technical information, when present in the articles, was generally correct, the panel found. This finding was surprising to several of the panelists, and deserves emphasis. In a highly technical field, a collection of general–interest articles produced mostly by general–assignment reporters contained few technical errors. Factual accuracy is a fundamental goal of journalism. By and large, the archive shows, this goal was achieved.

By contrast, the panel was critical of the archive for frequent "sins of omission." At the Environmental Risk Reporting Symposium on October 4, 1985, where the panel presented the results of its study, all agreed that incompleteness was the biggest problem with articles on environmental risk. The page-by-page notes the experts took while reading reflect the incompleteness of the articles. Comments such as "I'd like to know a lot more about this" and "nowhere does it mention that . . ." are common. "I see relatively few errors . . . see more holes in the stories," commented the journalist, who added that the reason reporters do not put information in stories is because they do not really understand the issues themselves: "A reporter will say, 'well, I don't really know what a PCB is but it was in a past clip so I'm going to put it in.' Part of it's laziness, part of it is a lack of time, but they don't ask fundamental questions."

As could be expected, the scientist noticed more errors and was more bothered by them than the other members of the panel. His comments:

> What I feel is happening is that the reporter is in the middle of the article, and he's going full steam and he doesn't have that particular item right at his fingertips, and he decides he's going to write what he thinks it means. . . . For example, it is an inaccuracy to describe PCBs being used in transformers as lubricants. . . . They don't lubricate anything. . . . My point is simply that with a little more effort, with a little more availability of the information, that kind of situation could be minimized. . . .[I] don't believe this is a deliberate misleading, it is a careless misleading.

The journalist attributed the relatively small number of errors in the articles to the "self-correcting mechanism" of reporting: "Reporters learn pretty quick if you get a fact—especially in an area like environmental issues where there is a pro and con—if you get something wrong the other side is going to pounce on you right away and say that person doesn't know what he's talking about."

Clarity/Understandability/Interest/Writing Quality

The panel found that jargon was often used by reporters at the expense of clarity. (Please refer to the discussion of *Tone* in an earlier section of this chapter.) Articles frequently lacked interest when the reporter had not succeeded in translating technical material into a form that was palatable to the average reader. The industry representative noted: "The writing style and the ability of the reporter to understand what he's doing and put it down logically and clearly for you is important for the average reader who has a time and attention span of five minutes."

The panel agreed that much of the writing was dull, that "more colorful quotes, interesting anecdotes" would have added greatly to the articles' readability. Even the most enterprising research pieces tended to be so tedious in their style that the panel found them extremely difficult to wade through.

Members of the panel agreed that the anecdotes, drama, and good quotes that contribute so much to the quality of an article are hard to get, and that it is especially difficult for reporters on the smaller daily newspapers to find provocative material. The industry representative called environmental reporting "the toughest of the disciplines. . . . This is tough to write about, and it's tough to find good stories . . . because little newspapers aren't going to have a big file of hazardous waste stuff. . . ."

However, the panelists also felt that reporters may not put a priority on making their articles exciting because they themselves are not inspired by the subject matter. The journalist commented:

> Most of these [articles] are from relatively small papers, and this is where reporters get their start. . . . First you don't have much room to write, you write a 300–word story, and you're reporting on the latest development in a landfill battle, basically the information is pretty boring. . . . It's an ongoing legal development so there's not a lot of room to write well. . . . It's not any kind of showcase for your writing.

The journalist was the toughest of all the panelists on the reporters, and the most critical of the writing quality, saying that, out of each "packet" of fifty or so stories, "there are only two or three that are really well done." He found many of the stories "terribly written . . . confusing . . . murky," saying "badly written to me is where . . . you're left wondering what the reporter means by this. . . . [There are] a lot of holes in the reporting. . . . Reporters aren't asking the fundamental questions."

Others on the panel cited editors as having equal responsibility for the overall quality of the articles, feeling that "the editing and placing of information" in a story is crucial. As the industry representative commented:

> If . . . the best part of [the story] is in the last four paragraphs . . . I'll bet 75% of the readers never saw that. . . . The well–written ones are compact. . . . There's a lot of waste in many of these—that's an editing problem. The reporter should know how to write a tight story, but the editor should know how to tighten it.

There was a consensus among the panel that there were not enough graphics, maps, charts, and, as the journalist put it, "things that help visualize . . . [for example] a map showing where landfills are." The activist said that he thought sources should be supplying more of this kind of material; the journalist commented that newspapers would use outside source visual aids only if the source was clearly identified on the bottom. Additionally, the journalist felt that high quality computer–generated graphics would soon be within the reach of smaller newspapers.

Enterprise

The most enterprising reporting was done on the longer stories, or in series, where the reporter had longer than the usual one–day deadline to research his or her story. The panelists agreed that general assignment reporters going out to cover an environmental story are not likely to be as enterprising as those whose specialty is the environment. Also, an environmental reporter is more likely to have background information, previous exposure to related issues, and contacts in the field at his or her fingertips. However, it should be noted that some general assignment reporters are writing quality stories on the environment, and a specialty in the environment is no guarantee that a particular reporter will be enterprising.

The journalist on the panel cited several articles in the archive as examples of solid, enterprising reporting. Among these were a special report done by the *Asbury Park Press*, "Troubled Waters"; *The News Tribune's* twelve–part series on Danish hazardous waste incinerator technology; "Spill Catcher" in *Today's Sunbeam*; and "State Probes Ciba Dumping" in the *Ocean County Observer*.[8] The journalist considered an item enterprising if the reporter had worked harder than normal to get a story, or had tracked down corporate records on the day a story broke, or had used some imagination in comparing the particular topic of the story with related issues, or had given a full, comprehensive account of a situation.

Unfortunately, being enterprising does not guarantee that an article is good. For example, although the panel found the *News Tribune* article cited above very enterprising—the reporters went to Denmark to study the technology and extrapolated that situation to Perth Amboy's—the article fell short in other areas. The experts on the panel called the final version of the story "puffery," and found it very one-sided.

The panel found that a few reporters consistently produced enterprising work—for example, James Dao of *The Daily Journal* and Janny Scott, then of *The Record* of Hackensack, N.J.

Newsworthiness

Because the archive is not a random sample, it is inappropriate to draw strong conclusions about newsworthiness from its content. A topic missing from the archive might or might not be underreported generally; we know only what editors provided when asked for a sample of their newspapers' best environmental risk reporting.

Nonetheless, the panelists were unanimous in their judgment that land-fill siting and the politics of landfills dominated the archive far more than they would have expected. This may be because New Jersey newspapers are focusing too much on landfills as opposed to other environmental stories, or it may be because New Jersey editors are particularly confident about their landfill stories or see them as most emblematic of environmental risk reporting. As the industry representative pointed out, many of the landfill stories in the archive were not focused on environmental risk at all:

> The overwhelming concentration on the landfill issue, story after story of confused and passionate attempts to extend, shut down or find alternatives to dump sites quite often—always, really—overshadowed the issue that orig-inally brought the problem to hand: a need to solve an immediate problem with dire consequences if it is not solved. Reporters seemed to avoid *that* story like the plague.

The panelists listed a number of serious environmental problems that were not strongly represented in the archive, including radioactive waste disposal, military waste, ocean disposal, pesticides and agricultural pollu-tion, non-point pollution sources, auto emissions, pathological waste, lia-bility insurance for victims of toxic waste poisoning, and innovative solutions to environmental problems that did not employ massive new facilities. The panel was unable to determine if these topics were treated, or how they were treated, in articles that were not submitted for the archive.

The panel speculated that some environmental issues may receive less coverage than landfills because they are less dramatic. The topics that were in the archive were covered, the journalist suggested, "because the problems show up immediately. . . . There's some people, they're squawking, they're upset about their water being polluted, and those are the ones that get the first media coverage." The activist agreed, saying "almost all [the topics not represented in the archive] are victimless; it's very difficult to identify people who have been hurt by them. These are longer term." Similarly, the scientist noted that many undramatic environmental problems are nonetheless causing serious environmental degradation:

> Municipal wastewater treatment plants . . . handle at least as much industrial sewage as those wastewater treatment plants devoted exclusively to industrial wastes. . . . There is no reference [in the archive] direct or implied as to the impact of municipal effluents on the environment. Non–point source discharges are the most uncontrolled discharges in the nation today. Automobiles and trucks contribute over 50% of the air emissions in the state of New Jersey today. There was nothing in the archive on this subject—it is not news.

The panel's criticism of the archive for lacking certain topics must be seen as very tentative; we have no evidence as to whether or not these topics were covered in the articles omitted from the archive. More useful is the panel's conviction that it is the responsibility of those who control what goes into the papers—the reporters and especially the editors—to find out what environmental issues are important and what environmental risks need to be understood. These will not always be the issues that are most dramatic, most obviously clamoring for attention. The extent to which newsworthiness should be defined by substantive importance or by public visibility is a familiar problem to journalists.

Resources/Geography/Individual Differences

The experts did not find significant differences among the work of large newspapers and small ones, or among newspapers in different regions of the state. One expert pointed out that in certain areas where there are more environmental hazards, there is a greater need for newspapers to report more detailed information about these problems. Also, as pointed out previously, one expert felt that landfill stories in particular, especially on smaller papers where they would be more likely to be covered by a general assignment reporter, tended to be dull and lacking in risk coverage.

Notes

1. Pat Politano, "Neighbors Have Mixed Views on Plant Siting," *Herald News*, 8 December 1984.
2. John MacKenna, "Iron Adds Stress to City Lives," *News Tribune*, 27 February 1984.
3. Chris Biddle, "Leaks," *Burlington County Times*, 24–27 June 1984.
4. James Dao, "Self-regulation Insufficient for Controlling Spills," *Daily Journal*, [Elizabeth, N.J.], June 1984.
5. Joseph Fisher, "Dioxin Fears Haunt Passaic County," *The News* [Paterson, N.J.], 6 June 1983.
6. Don Bennett, "Chemical Dumping Checked," *Ocean County Observer*, 19 April 1984.
7. Janny Scott, "New Jersey Safe from Such Disaster?" *The Record* [Hackensack, N.J.], 6 December 1984.
8. Si Liberman, ed., "Troubled Waters," *Asbury Park Press*, 6 May 1984, special editorial report. Kathleen Casey, Lois DiTommaso, and Charles Paolino, "From Denmark to Perth Amboy?" *The News Tribune* [Woodbridge, N.J.], 12–26 November 1984. John Hayes, "Spill Catcher," *Today's Sunbeam*, 30 November 1984. Don Bennett, "Chemical Dumping Checked," *Ocean County Observer*, 19 April 1984.

4

How Good is the Best?

In spite of the vast differences in methodology between the content analysis and the expert analysis, there were many common findings. In fact, in many cases where the content analysis demonstrated a particular trend quantitatively, the expert analysis supplied the insight and depth to the finding to make it that much more meaningful.

Perhaps the most significant of these common findings was the scarcity of explicit risk information in articles that are ostensibly about environmental risk. The content analysis showed that nearly 70% of the paragraphs in the archive do not discuss risk at all. Of course, this in itself is not an indictment of reporters; there are many topics to cover in an environmental article—blame, cost, background information—and, unless an environmental risk is imminent, this other information is generally more newsworthy than risk information. Thus, looking at the numbers, 30% of the paragraphs devoted to environmental risk may seem just about right.

The experts, however, felt very strongly that environmental risk is not covered as much as it should be. Their impressions of the archive were, basically, that the risk information which needed to be talked about in environmental articles was simply not there.

Possible reasons for this have been mentioned already: (1) that editors did not respond to the request for articles on environmental risk but rather sent articles dealing more broadly with environmental issues; (2) that risk is not "news" and hence takes a back seat to the events that are considered news; (3) that risk is too difficult to report on, and many general assignment reporters who do the environmental stories do not feel they have the background to report on risk; (4) that many experts, even those knowledgeable in toxicology, do not think primarily in terms of risk; (5) that experts who really know about risk are too difficult to contact in the short time a reporter has to write a story; (6) that risk information takes up too much space in an article and would get cut out when it crossed the editor's desk;

and (7) that reporters and editors share a conviction that readers do not want to wade through complex, tentative, technical data.

Each of these explanations is probably relevant to a certain degree. In general, the experts felt, reporters and editors seemed not so much unable as disinclined to provide more than the most basic risk information. In case after case the experts asked for more information or felt an article had not gone far enough in explaining the risk aspects of an environmental situation. Many articles, they felt, were "half–done," and even those articles that were particularly enterprising, the experts found, did not have the basic risk information they felt should be presented. The experts' impression of the archive was that the reporters and the editors were simply not asking thorough questions about risk.

The experts also felt that there seemed to be an assumption on the part of the reporters and editors that the reading public already knows the risk information so they (the reporters) do not need to cover it again. One of the experts noted that risk is often mentioned casually, as if the references are obvious and well–known to the readers, particularly in cases of landfill siting or cleanup, and other ongoing stories which reporters assume readers have followed from the beginning. Often the stories treated risk as a dichotomy. Having duly noted that a particular substance or situation was hazardous, reporters seemed disinclined to pursue the complex and difficult follow–up: How hazardous? Under what conditions?

Both the experts and the numbers agreed that when environmental risk information was reported, it was more alarming than reassuring. Of the total paragraphs in the archive, 10.0% assert that a substance or situation is risky and another 10.2% assert that the hazardous substance or situation is present, as opposed to 3.2% that say not risky and 2.3% that say not present. The experts, too, found that the archive created the impression that the world is a scary place and that New Jersey's environmental problems are very grave. Interestingly, the experts were not angered at the alarming imbalance in environmental risk coverage (though three of the four felt that reality was less dangerous than the coverage portrayed). The experts attributed the imbalance not to bias but to the conventions of journalism—risk is more newsworthy than safety—and they seemed almost fatalistic about its inevitability.

By far the scariest aspect of most of the articles is the headlines, according to the experts. They felt that there were too many misleading headlines (and to a lesser extent leads) that created a feeling of doom that is hard to shake, particularly when many people do not read much except the headline and a few paragraphs.

Although the formal content analysis did not include headlines, the analysis of the articles found very little difference between the thrust of risk content in the early paragraphs and the thrust of later paragraphs. The early information, however, is more likely to be unattributed. It seems likely that sourceless, broad assertions of risk early in a story may set a tone that survives regardless of later details and qualifiers.

Another reason the articles give an overall scary impression, according to the experts, is their failure to follow–up and their tendency to avoid technical details. This, the experts felt, may well create anxiety in the reader. For example, an article that asserts that the air is safe to breathe after a fire or a spill but also says that five people are in the hospital because they inhaled something toxic is guilty of an error in chronology that leaves people wondering "should I go outside or shouldn't I?" Indeed, it is important to note that an article that quotes one source saying a risk is negligible and another saying it is huge does not leave the reader comfortably in the middle. Instead, the predictable responses for many readers are frustration, uncertainty, distrust, paralysis, and alarm. When sources disagree in this way, the reporter is not responsible for the result—but the result may be a bewildered and anxious public.

It is possible that the conventions of journalism are incompatible to some extent with the realities of environmental risk. Reporters often pursue balanced coverage by quoting extreme views on both sides, rather than by quoting sources with more moderate views or by including more details and qualifiers. There are good reasons for this: extreme views are clearer and more interesting; conflict generates more drama than moderate views; and sources in the middle are less likely to seek media attention. The content analysis finding that intermediate paragraphs on risk are relatively uncommon, and the expert analysis finding that details about risk are relatively uncommon both testify to reporters' and editors' preference for assertive, clear–cut quotations. This approach works admirably for articles about politics, including environmental politics. It works less well for articles about environmental risk—which may help explain why the expert panel felt there was too much political reporting and too little risk reporting in the archive.

Uninvolved experts are not being used as much as they should be for information about risk, according to both the experts and the numbers. In the analysis of the overall distribution of sources in the archive, uninvolved experts were found to be quoted in only 4.2% of the paragraphs, less than all other sources except workers. Even at the article level, experts trailed behind state government, local government, general government, and industry, and experts tended to be cited later in stories than government sources. None of this is surprising when one considers that the archive contains relatively little information that directly assesses risk. But the risk information that does exist in the archive is largely from industry, government, and unattributed sources. Experts contributed well under ten percent of the risk information in the archive.

The panel felt that the reliance on sources other than outside experts for risk information was basically a problem of accessibility. Government sources and industry spokespeople are reached more easily than experts, who may have to be ferreted out—which often takes more time than a reporter has to devote to a story. The panel felt that many reporters simply do not know who the experts are, and do not make the extra effort to find out. The general impression the panel garnered from the archive was that reporters are trying to make environmental reporting fit into a black–and–white pattern of reporting that, say, political reporting follows, and tend not to look for or notice other sources that might enrich their stories. Interestingly, the content analysis showed that when reporters did cite experts about risk, their comments tended to be no less alarming and somewhat *more* extreme than the comments of other sources; the stereotyped reassuring, inconclusive expert was not much in evidence.

The panel judged that when bias existed in the archive, it was less likely to be intentional than simply a matter of a reporter not taking the time to seek out alternative sources or dissenting opinions to find out what the other side—if there was one—had to say. The result was a heavy reliance on a most quoted source. The content analysis illustrates how easily this can occur in the source–by–risk analyses (see chapter 2). These analyses show that certain sources are more likely to take a particular stance on risk—for example, advocacy groups are much more likely to say a situation is risky than not risky, while industry is far more likely to deny risk than to assert it; similarly, state and county government sources tended to be more alarming than federal and local government sources. As a result, articles that relied too heavily on one source would necessarily lean in one direction. However, as pointed out earlier in the discussion, the tendency of reporters to want to achieve objectivity by contrasting both sides may sometimes lead to the reader's confusion. In many cases, then, it may serve the reader best to add more background details and more moderate opinions to the mix.

It should be noted here that, while the problems discussed thus far have focused on reporters, the panel felt strongly that the "buck stops" at the editor's desk, and that if reporters are sometimes guilty of careless or lazy reporting, editors have the responsibility to question and correct it. In many enterprising articles in the archive, bad editing—not enough editing, poor placement of key paragraphs, headlines and leads that misrepresented content, and lack of follow–up—prevented the article from achieving the excellence its enterprise merited. The experts also pointed out that some of the best environmental risk reporting comes in series and special sections that do not command the readership of a front-page hard news article. They urged editors to ask for more risk information in hard news. (To corroborate this recommendation, the content analysis did find more risk information in background stories than in hard news.) The overall feeling was that in many cases editors are not meeting their responsibilities.

While the expert panel felt that risk information was placed too late in stories to be of any use to the average reader who does not read that far, the content analysis found risk information distributed fairly evenly throughout the story. These findings do not necessarily disagree, however. It appears that many environmental risk articles begin with unattributed paragraphs that simply assert a situation is risky—which agrees with the panel's findings that leads are often scary and misleading in tone. The details about the risk—the standards, expert opinions, and so forth—are placed towards the end, past the point where most people have stopped reading. The net effect is that people are reading the scary declarative statements about risk and are not getting the explanation of how much risk, who says the risk is real, who agrees and disagrees with the information about the risk—either because it comes too late or because it is not there at all.

One aspect of the archive that the content analysis could not address was accuracy. Though the experts did find some technical errors in the archive, only a few were judged truly serious; most were matters of incompleteness or oversimplification rather than actual errors. Of course, as the panel pointed out, any error is serious in a news story, not only because it misleads readers but perhaps more importantly because it alienates well-informed sources that could be used by reporters. The panel urged reporters to check technical facts as carefully as possible, and to seek answers from experts rather than extrapolating from the facts at hand. However, they also congratulated the reporters and editors responsible for stories in the archive for covering a complex technical topic with relatively few errors. The challenge now, they felt, is to incorporate more technical information without falling into technical error.

Tone, like accuracy, was assessed by the expert panel but not by the formal content analysis. An inappropriate or misleading tone, the panel felt, tended to occur when reporters tried to translate scientific jargon into simpler language (for example, "discharging" versus "dumping"). While trying to simplify terms so that readers can more easily understand them is desirable, the panel felt that frequently reporters use words that do not quite fit the situation. The panel conceded that this was sometimes unavoidable and that reporters were in a bind—whether to leave the technical terms in and lose many of the readers, or translate them to more familiar but possibly more alarming words. The panel did feel, however, that report-ers were taking too much license with technical terms, and that more interpretation by experts was appropriate.

The central theme in both the content analysis and the expert analysis of the archive is the need for more risk information, especially technical background (as opposed to unsubstantiated opinion). The Environmental Risk Reporting Project therefore decided to study the feasibility of various options for providing risk information to the media during breaking sto-ries. Phase Two reports the results of this research.

PHASE TWO

EXPLORING WAYS TO IMPROVE NEWS COVERAGE OF ENVIRONMENTAL RISK

5

Methods for Determining the Attitudes of Environmental Reporters and Their Sources

Acting on the assumption that reporters do not report as much background information in their environmental stories as they might—an assumption supported by analyzing the "best" New Jersey environmental reporting—the Environmental Risk Reporting Project set out to find why this is the case and what can be done about it.

A series of telephone interviews with environmental reporters at each of the twenty-six daily newspapers in New Jersey was followed up by mail surveys, in-person surveys at the Environmental Risk Reporting Symposium on October 4, 1985, and finally a simulated risk situation at the Symposium where reporters "covered" a breaking environmental story. Industry and government representatives also were interviewed as to their attitudes about environmental risk reporting, and about the feasibility of a number of options proposed by the project for providing environmental risk information to the media.

The interviews and surveys differed in style and in specific wording of questions, but all were concerned with the following issues:

1. *The reporters' perceived need for risk information and their problems in obtaining it.* Do reporters really want more background material? Would they use it if it were available? From what sources do reporters most want to get risk information? Under what circumstances do they want it? Do they want it on the first day of a breaking story or are they satisfied with covering risk aspects of an environmental situation in subsequent reports? Are they currently having problems getting the information they want?

2. *The feasibility of various options for providing risk information to the media.* What type of information could each proposed service offer to reporters? How often would each service be used? Would the informa-

tion provided by each proposed service be in a form that reporters would use? Which service would provide the best access to information? Would the use of the service justify the cost of implementing it?

Telephone Interviews

For the initial telephone interviews, reporters were identified in two ways: (1) names that appeared repeatedly as by–lines in the archive, and (2) recommendations from editors and other reporters.

Editors were interviewed if they showed a strong interest in the project or if a particular newspaper did not have a designated environmental reporter. (On some papers, all reporters on staff were expected to cover the environment if they were assigned it.) In all, thirty–eight journalists—thirty reporters and eight editors—were interviewed.

A typical interview lasted from forty–five minutes to one hour. Topics covered during that time included:

1. *Environmental news coverage:* How does your newspaper cover breaking environmental stories? Are reporters sent on–site? If so, how many and under what circumstances? How many of these incidents does your paper cover in a year? Is a breaking environmental story covered differently than other environmental stories? How? Why?
2. *Sources/information availability:* Who are your major sources during a breaking story? For other environmental stories? During an environmental emergency, do you have trouble getting the information you want? During a non–emergency?
3. *References:* What reference materials do you have in the newsroom to help you report an environmental story? Are you familiar with the Scientists' Institute for Public Information (SIPI)? Have you ever used SIPI's Media Resource Service?
4. *Team/hotline:* Would an on–site source of background information help you report environmental risk stories? Would a hotline? What kind of information would you want from either of these services? How else could the Environmental Risk Reporting Project help you report these stories?
5. *Reporters' background:* How long have you been covering environmental risk stories? How often do you go on–site? Do you have any formal science or environmental education? If not, do you think that this hinders your reporting of environmental stories? What is your main beat?

Most journalists did not have to be prompted with specific questions but spoke about all the areas outlined above after the interviewer explained the goals of the survey. The same issues were discussed in all interviews, however, whether the questions were raised by the interviewer or by the journalist.

Additional interviews were conducted with emergency responders; federal, state, and county government officials; industry representatives; academic scientists; and environmental activists who were identified from lists or recommended to the project by journalists. These individuals supplied insights unique to their positions as sources and newsmakers, and added a different dimension to information obtained from journalists. These interviews were concerned with the following issues:

1. *Role as a news source:* Are you comfortable with this role? Do reporters ask for environmental risk information? If not, do you give it anyway? What other information do reporters ask for? Is the information reporters want for a breaking story different than for a non–emergency story?
2. *Environmental news reporting:* Does environmental reporting need to be improved in New Jersey? How can it be improved? Would making more background information available to reporters help? Does it matter if this information is presented on or off–site? Are some types of stories better than others? What makes this difference?
3. *Feedback on options being considered by the project:* What equipment is necessary and recommended? How much does it cost? What reference books and computer data bases are available and useful? What are the problems with these?
4. *The emergency scene:* What should team members expect at the scene? How should they be trained? What safety equipment and precautions are necessary? What information is available on–site? How often do these emergencies occur and how long do they last?

Of particular help were groups that had experience operating a hotline or providing on–site media services. A complete list of journalists and non–journalists interviewed is provided in Appendix C.

Mail Survey

The thirty–eight journalists who were interviewed over the telephone were asked if they would be willing to complete a more detailed mail survey. In the first part of the survey, the journalists were asked to rate sixty–three categories of information relative to their importance in a first–day breaking story. They were given three choices:

1. The information is important and urgent.
2. The information is important, but not necessarily for a first–day story.
3. The information is less important.

Journalists were also instructed to circle any item they were currently having difficulty finding for their breaking stories.

The sixty–three items were divided into six groups as follows:

1. *General information:* What is the name of the chemical involved? Where is it manufactured? Does it occur naturally in the environment?
2. *Health and environmental effects:* Does it affect human health? Does it increase the likelihood of cancer? Does it increase the likelihood of birth defects?
3. *Chemical behavior:* Is it water–soluble? Is it flammable? Is it corrosive? Can it explode? What is its LD-50?
4. *Company or agency responsible:* What is the telephone number? Address? President's name? Company lawsuit record? Does the company have an emergency response plan?
5. *Surrounding environment:* Is the substance or situation near drinking water sources? What is the local community like? How many people live nearby? Is it near a school, hospital, or nursing home?
6. *Legal:* Who has jurisdiction over the site? What permits are required? What "lists" is the chemical on? Who is responsible for the cleanup?

Journalists were then asked to provide information regarding the amount of time they spent covering environmental stories.

Next, journalists were asked to rate the options that were being considered by the project at that time: the Mobile Environmental Risk Information Team and the hotline. They were requested to rate the team—enormously useful, useful, or marginally useful—and then rate the hotline relative to the team: much less useful (than the team), somewhat less useful, slightly less useful, just as useful, or even better (than the team). Journalists then characterized their relative satisfaction in getting answers from experts for their breaking stories in five categories from very satisfied to very dissatisfied.

Finally, comments and suggestions were solicited from the respondents. The survey form and cover letter are contained in Appendix D.

All thirty–eight journalists interviewed by telephone agreed to complete the mail–in survey. Twenty–nine actually responded. Based on these responses it appears that the environmental reporting experience varies from a part–time role to a half–time assignment. A full–time environmental beat is rare even in New Jersey.

Of the twenty–nine who responded, fourteen said they spent less than 10% of their time reporting on environmental risk, seven spent between 11% and 25% of their time reporting on environmental risk, four spent 26% to 50% of their time covering environmental risk, and one reporter devoted over 50% of his or her reporting time on the subject. Three journalists (two of them editors) did not specify their involvement in environmental risk reporting.

Conference Survey

Journalists who attended the project's Environmental Risk Reporting Symposium at the University of Medicine and Dentistry of New Jersey—Robert Wood Johnson Medical School on October 4, 1985 were asked to fill out a survey that asked the following three questions: (1) How do you feel about the need for background health risk information in a breaking story? (2) Where do you think health risk information belongs: in a breaking story, in a sidebar to the breaking story, in a second–day follow–up, or in an in–depth feature? (3) Which two of the four options listed for providing background information would you prefer: an environmental library, a hotline, a wire service for specific health risk information, or a Mobile Environmental Risk Information Team?

Note that by this time, through feedback obtained from the telephone interviews and the mail survey, two more options for providing risk information had been added: the environmental library and the wire service.

There were a total of seventeen responses from journalists at the conference: four environmental reporters; three general assignment reporters; two statehouse reporters; two municipal reporters; one county reporter; one crime reporter; one business reporter; one science/energy reporter; one municipal/environmental reporter; and one editor.

The conference survey can be found in Appendix E.

Simulation

Information about what facts reporters want for a breaking story and who they want them from was also gathered from a simulated emergency exercise reporters participated in at the Symposium. A fire at a supermarket warehouse containing toxic materials (normal household items that can be found at today's supermarket) was "covered" by reporters as if they were working against a real deadline. During the role–playing exercise, various officials were on hand "at the scene" or available "by telephone" to answer any questions the reporters had.

The sources reporters chose to speak to and the questions they asked were recorded. A list of participants, a description of the scenario, and instructions for the simulation can be found in Appendix F.

6

Attitudes toward Environmental Risk Information

As stated previously, the goals of this research were twofold: (1) to investigate why background environmental risk information is not appearing in breaking stories concerned with environmental risk emergencies, and (2) to get feedback from reporters and others regarding the project's proposals for making risk information more readily available. This chapter deals with the first of these two goals.

Here, then, are the project's findings regarding existing attitudes about risk information, arranged in terms of the methods used to arrive at these results.

Interviews with Journalists

The interviews conducted with journalists yielded immediate insights as to why background risk information is not common in breaking stories. Most of those interviewed said that environmental health risk information is simply not seen—by reporters or editors—as a first-day issue.

Judy Petsonk of the *Courier–Post* (Camden–Cherry Hill, New Jersey) said that, for the most part, environmental reporters are not even sent to cover environmental emergencies. "There's a sense that there are deadline reporters and police reporters," she explained, "and they are not connected with environmental reporters." As a result, in an environmental emergency the emphasis in coverage is on the emergency, not the environment.

When they are sent to cover environmental emergencies, moreover, reporters said they tend to report the facts of the emergency. William Terdoslavich of the *North Jersey Advance* (Dover, New Jersey) said that on the first day "you just want to find out what happened," and that the environmental angle could wait until a follow–up story. Brad Rudin of the Passaic

Herald News agreed: "Generally in these emergencies it's the basic five W's that get in [the story]."

In large part, the tendency to favor the details of the emergency over the health risk details is journalistic tradition; journalists have typically been trained to cover emergencies, and that is what they feel comfortable doing. Also, they know the public wants to know how the fire started, how many got hurt, etc.

The interviews also left the impression that sources were a problem for reporters in obtaining the risk information they wanted. Many reporters complained about not being able to locate "official sources"—the state government was cited most often—to find out the extent of the environmental risk. John Hudzinski, an editor for the *Asbury Park Press*, said that the New Jersey Department of Environmental Protection (DEP) is often "uncooperative," that the DEP takes a long time to get back with answers or does not have the information. Fran Sheehan of the *Vineland Times Journal* and the *Millville Daily* agreed: "DEP and every other state agency has a very inefficient system of getting information out." Sheehan said she had trouble obtaining information when working on an investigative piece, and that many times she could not even find out who was in charge of a certain area or office.

In spite of the difficulty reporters seem to have getting in touch with official sources, they were unanimous that they preferred state government—and occasionally local government—sources over non–government expert sources for information on a breaking story. Analysis of the archive corroborates this trend (please refer to chapter 2). In the analysis of the sources used by reporters for different types of articles (for example, hard news, feature, background, and investigative), state, local, and county governments were used more than any other source for hard news stories, and were used more for hard news stories than for any other type of article. State government, for example, was cited in 18.6% of the paragraphs in hard news stories, versus 11.0% of the paragraphs in features. County government was used as a source in 9.7% of the hard news paragraphs, versus 2.2% of the feature paragraphs. Local government was cited in 12.4% of the hard news paragraphs and 4.1% of the feature paragraphs. Overall, government at all levels accounted for 37.0% of all paragraph attributions in the archive, and 47.9% of the hard news paragraphs (please refer to Table 2.10).

In fairness to the state in its role as a source for environmental risk information, it is important to mention that the kind of risk information reporters want generally falls into two categories: the immediate "how much of the hazardous substance is in the air?" and the follow–up "how much of this substance can cause problems?" Reporters' complaints about the inefficiency of state officials in providing timely information often refer to test results that are almost impossible to obtain in the time frame that reporters need them. According to Jim Staples, public information officer for the New Jersey Department of Environmental Protection: "In the final analysis, during the time of turmoil, there is very little solid information in terms of what's there. . . ."

If information about the concentration of chemicals in the air or water were available on-site at a fire or spill, reporters might be more inclined to use other background risk information in their breaking stories; for example, if they could report how much of a substance was present, they would be more inclined to report the standards and the risk involved. As it stands now, however, reporters are being told that officials do not know what the substance is or what the levels are. As a result, they cannot speculate on the risks associated with an unknown and so they report what *is* known: the five W's. (Reporters covering a chronic risk situation—a landfill or pesticide spraying controversy, for example—are more likely to have access to the relevant risk information. Even in these cases coverage often stresses politics, cost, and other issues more than risk. Please refer to chapter 2.)

It follows from these observations that reporters are unlikely to add much background information about risk to first-day breaking stories, no matter what new services are provided to make the information more accessible. Improved access to background information is likely to improve the quality of such information in second-day stories (when events are important enough to deserve second-day coverage), and in feature, background, and investigative stories. But to expect a great deal of background information about risk in a first-day hard news story on an environmental emergency is to expect a significant change in the way journalists view their job.

Interviews with Non-Journalists

The majority of the non-journalists interviewed shared the impression that reporters are working as hard as they can to get information for stories about environmental risk. The most common problem that sources had with reporters was that reporters were on the scene at an emergency situation asking questions for which no answers were available. According to David Palmer, president of the consulting firm Emergency Response Planning and Management, Inc.: "One of the most difficult things to deal with in a crisis is information. . . . It is difficult to get accurate information in a few minutes, or a few hours."

Experience, especially at one newspaper, seems to play an important part in non-journalists' attitudes toward reporters. According to Lester Jargowsky of the Monmouth County Health Department: "There are different kinds of reporters. If they've been with that particular paper . . . for awhile and are experienced, they're easy to work with." Jargowsky stated that a problem with environmental coverage is the rapid turnover of reporters; when reporters are new, he said, they simply do not have the necessary background to cover environmental news. This can be "extremely annoying" to sources, according to Jargowsky. Robert Ferraiuolo of the Hudson County Regional Health Commission said that he gives a new reporter one chance, and if he or she gets the details of the story wrong, he will not deal with that particular reporter again.

There is variation among sources as to how they convey risk information to reporters. Some sources volunteer information; in fact, some find that they give the reporters more than they ask for. Ferraiuolo stated that when reporters do not ask what he feels are the correct risk questions (for example, what happens when the substance burns, what the reaction products are, and how dangerous the products are) he and his staff will tell them, "This is what you need to know." Ferraiuolo said that reporters are good at asking the basic questions, but that they do not always follow-up with the "second string" of questions regarding risk.

Jim Staples, public information officer for the New Jersey Department of Environmental Protection, also felt that many reporters did not ask the appropriate questions, and that the reason for this was that they lacked training in the environmental issues. "You might train him [the reporter] ahead of time to be better able to deal with an environmental situation," he stated. "They [reporters] might as well have a few hours of some kind of seminar to help them deal with it at the time, and they would have a much broader framework of reference to relate it to what's going on in the surrounding community."

Although some sources were eager to give information on risk to reporters, there was a sense in many of the interviews that neither the reporters *nor* the sources put a high premium on getting detailed background risk information into breaking stories. The emphasis during the time a story is breaking is on the immediate effects. David Palmer made a distinction between an immediate crisis, such as a transportation accident, and a developing emergency. A crisis situation, he said, "wouldn't be the time to deal with the press. . . . It's important that the public do what they have to do to protect themselves without knowing why." In a slowly developing emergency, on the other hand, Palmer said the press could be brought in earlier. He advocated a press room where officials and experts could meet with the press to "give out correct information as it is available," but said that while the crisis is developing, "I don't believe that they [reporters] should be telling the public the risk information at that point." He said that people in a crisis situation did not need to know that X chemical would cause *Y* number of cancers. "I don't want them dealing with that while a vapor cloud is approaching their house," he said.

Mail Survey

As compared to the telephone interviews, the mail survey asked very specific questions to ferret out reporters' attitudes about including specific risk information in their stories and whether or not they were having problems obtaining the information. Twenty–nine journalists responded to the survey. Even though this sample is small, the survey shows trends in reporter attitudes that corroborate the findings of much of the project's other research.

Desirability of Information—Need to Know

Table 6.1 summarizes journalists' survey responses. Note that while respondents could categorize each type of information as "important and urgent," "important but not urgent" (appropriate for a second–day story), or "less important," very little use was made of the "less important" category. In fact, the greatest number of journalists identifying *any* item as "less important" was ten (34% of the twenty–nine respondents)—for information about the experimental dose capable of killing 50% of an animal population. For most items, only one or two journalists checked "less important." Since some of the items in the survey are in fact extremely infrequent in newspaper articles, it seems fair to conclude that journalists are simply reluctant ever to say they do not want a piece of information, however unlikely they may be to use it. In any case, the useful distinction in the survey was between the items journalists want for a first–day story and the items they do not need until a follow–up story.

A notable finding emerging from this survey was that reporters tend to want basic human health risk information for their breaking stories, but not supporting details or non–human effects. For example, in the general information category, twenty–eight of the twenty–nine journalists surveyed (97%) wanted to know the name of the chemical for their breaking stories. Twenty–five (86%) were interested in levels the chemical is permitted to reach in the environment or the workplace, and twenty–four (83%) wanted to include the chemical's use. In the health and environmental effects category, all twenty–nine respondents wanted to know what impact, if any, the chemical has on humans, and twenty–six (90%) felt that the acute effects of skin and eye irritation were important and urgent; twenty–five (86%) were interested in whether the substance increases the cancer rate. By contrast, only eighteen (62%) wanted to know what kind of cancer or if the substance increased the likelihood of genetic mutation. Only thirteen (45%) were interested in whether the substance occurred naturally in the environment, and only ten (35%) wanted to know at what levels.

Supporting evidence was not in heavy demand by reporters for their first–day breaking stories. While twenty–two respondents (76%) felt that the amount of the chemical that could cause it to be hazardous was urgent, only seventeen (59%) wanted to know how serious a carcinogen the substance was, only twelve (41%) were interested in whether or not scientists were sure the substance was a carcinogen, and only eight (28%) felt that reporting what studies were done to show the substance was a carcinogen was important for the breaking story.

Although a chemical's adverse effect on wildlife and plants could be an indicator of a possible threat to human health, most of the reporters surveyed would not put this information into a breaking story. Only seven (24%) said they felt a chemical's effect on wildlife and plants was important and urgent enough for a first–day story. Only six (21%) felt that the effect of the substance on aquatic life merited space in their breaking story. In fact, damage to property (thirteen or 45%) and the community infrastructure (sixteen or 55%) were considered urgent by more reporters than the effect on wildlife, reflecting a greater concern for reporting economic factors than non–human environmental effects.

In the category of chemical behavior, by far the most urgent and important facts for reporters were the obvious physical characteristics. For the first–day breaking story, twenty–eight reporters (97%) said they wanted to know whether the chemical was explosive or flammable, whether it could travel from the site of the accident, and, if so, how it could travel. Twenty–seven (93%) felt it was urgent to know if the chemical was a solid, liquid, or gas, and twenty–two (76%) would include corrosivity in the breaking story. Less important for the breaking story, according to the respondents, was whether the chemical was biodegradable (fifteen or 52%) and how persistent it was in the environment (eighteen or 62%).

While twenty–six (90%) felt that it was urgent to know if the chemical could get into the local water supply, only twelve (41%) felt it was urgent to report whether or not it was water–soluble. Only nine (31%) felt it was urgent to report in the breaking story whether the chemical was fat–soluble, even though the survey form explained that "fat–soluble" meant the chemical could be stored in human tissue. The LD–50 (the dose capable of killing half an animal population) would be used by only ten (35%) of the journalists for their breaking stories.

Concerning the company or agency responsible, reporters unanimously felt that a phone number was urgent. (Note that this category includes items that reporters would need to cover the story but would not neces-

TABLE 6.1
Reporters' Attitudes toward Specific Risk Information (n = 29)**

Item	Item Important and Urgent	Difficulty Getting Info.	Item Important but Not Urgent	Difficulty Getting Info.	Item Less Important	Difficulty Getting Info.
I. CHEMICAL(S) INVOLVED IN INCIDENT						
A. General Information						
1. Name of chemical	28	(2)	1	(0)	0	(0)
2. Use	24	(1)	4	(1)	1	(0)
3. a. Occur naturally*	13	(0)	14	(0)	2	(0)
b. At what levels*	10	(1)	14	(1)	5	(0)
4. Permissible levels*	25	(7)	3	(1)	1	(0)
5. Where manufactured	16	(1)	12	(2)	1	(0)
6. Manufactured locally	16	(1)	12	(2)	1	(0)
B. Health and Environmental Effects*						
1. Impact on humans	29	(4)	0	(0)	0	(0)
2. Increase cancer	25	(4)	4	(2)	0	(0)
a. What type	18	(2)	9	(2)	2	(0)
b. What studies show	8	(1)	17	(4)	4	(2)
c. Are scientists sure	12	(2)	14	(3)	3	(2)
d. How serious	17	(7)	9	(0)	3	(1)
3. Genetic mutation	18	(6)	8	(1)	3	(0)
4. Birth defects	21	(7)	6	(0)	2	(0)
5. Irritate skin/eyes	26	(2)	3	(0)	0	(0)
6. How much is hazardous	22	(3)	6	(0)	1	(0)
7. Treatment after exposure	19	(1)	9	(0)	1	(0)
8. Effect on wildlife	7	(0)	18	(1)	4	(0)
9. Effect on aquatic life	6	(0)	18	(1)	5	(0)
10. Effect on plants	7	(0)	16	(0)	6	(0)

11. Long-term emotional effects	14	(2)	10	(2)	5	(0)
12. Property damage	13	(0)	12	(0)	4	(0)
13. Community infrastructure damage	16	(2)	10	(1)	3	(0)
C. Chemical Behavior						
1. Water soluble*	12	(0)	15	(2)	2	(0)
2. Get into local water*	26	(2)	2	(0)	1	(0)
3. Fat soluble*	9	(0)	14	(0)	6	(3)
4. Liquid, gas, solid	27	(0)	2	(0)	0	(0)
5. Can it travel from site*	28	(1)	0	(0)	1	(0)
6. How does it travel*	28	(2)	1	(0)	0	(0)
7. Explosive*	28	(1)	1	(0)	1	(0)
8. Flammable*	28	(1)	0	(0)	1	(1)
9. Corrosive*	22	(1)	6	(2)	2	(0)
10. Biodegradable*	15	(1)	12	(1)	2	(0)
11. How persistent*	18	(1)	9	(2)		(0)
12. LD-50*	10	(1)	9	(0)	10	(1)
13. Reporter precautions	22	(3)	3	(0)	4	(0)
II. COMPANY OR AGENCY RESPONSIBLE						
1. Telephone number	29	(4)	0	(0)	0	(0)
2. Address	28	(0)	1	(0)	0	(0)
3. Size	14	(0)	10	(0)	5	(1)
4. Other locations	11	(3)	13	(0)	5	(1)
5. Night telephone number	28	(11)	0	(0)	1	(0)
6. President's name	16	(2)	8	(5)	5	(1)
7. Accident record	19	(7)	9	(5)	1	(1)
8. Lawsuit record	10	(6)	13	(0)	6	(2)
9. Owned by larger company	15	(1)	12	(0)	2	(0)
10. Emergency response plan	18	(4)	10	(0)	1	(0)
11. Who's responsible for emergency response plan	16	(4)	10	(0)	3	(0)

* Question related to environmental risk.
** The numbers in parentheses are subsets of the numbers reported to their left.

TABLE 6.1 (Continued)
Reporters' Attitudes toward Specific Risk Information (n = 29)**

Item	Item Important and Urgent	Difficulty Getting Info.	Item Important but Not Urgent	Difficulty Getting Info.	Item Less Important	Difficulty Getting Info.
III. SURROUNDING ENVIRONMENT						
1. Near drinking water	29	(0)	0	(0)	0	(0)
2. Near other waterways	24	(0)	4	(0)	1	(0)
3. Character of local community	12	(0)	14	(0)	3	(0)
4. People live nearby	26	(0)	1	(0)	2	(0)
5. Schools nearby	24	(0)	4	(0)	1	(0)
6. Hospitals, etc.	23	(0)	5	(0)	1	(0)
7. Near roadway or airport	23	(0)	5	(0)	1	(0)
8. Existing environ. problems	11	(1)	15	(0)	3	(1)
IV. LEGAL						
1. What gov't has jurisdiction	23	(2)	4	(0)	2	(0)
2. What are applicable laws	15	(5)	11	(1)	3	(0)
3. What permits	12	(3)	13	(2)	4	(0)
4. Laws governing liability	10	(1)	13	(3)	6	(2)
5. Listed under EPA, OSHA*	19	(4)	8	(1)	2	(0)
6. Laws that govern who pays	8	(1)	17	(1)	4	(0)
7. Who cleans up	18	(2)	9	(2)	2	(1)

* Question related to environmental risk.
** The numbers in parentheses are subsets of the numbers reported to their left.

sarily use in their articles.) The next most important and urgent items for reporters were the address of the company in question and a night telephone number for the company (twenty–eight or 97%). Somewhat less urgent for reporters to know in order to cover a breaking story were the accident record of the company (nineteen or 66%), whether the company had an emergency response plan (eighteen or 62%), the names of the company president and the person responsible for the emergency response plan (sixteen or 55%), and other details about the company.

Reporters were relatively interested in the population that could be affected by an emergency situation for their breaking stories. All twenty–nine felt it was important and urgent to know if the substance or situation was near a drinking water source. Twenty–six (90%) wanted to know how many people lived near the site of the incident. Twenty–four (83%) felt it was urgent and important to know if the emergency situation was near schools, and twenty–three (79%) wanted to know for their breaking stories if there were hospitals or nursing homes, or highways or airports nearby. Only eleven (38%) felt it was urgent to know other environmental problems in the area.

Legal information seemed less important to journalists for the first–day breaking story. Twenty–three reporters (79%) wanted to know what municipal government had jurisdiction over the problem site, nineteen (66%) felt it was urgent and important to know what lists the chemical in question was on, and eighteen (62%) wanted to know who would be responsible for the cleanup. Fifteen (52%) wanted to know what regulations the particular chemical fell under for manufacturing, storage, and transportation; twelve (41%) thought it was urgent to know what permits were required; ten (35%) wanted to know the laws that determined liability for the accident; and eight (28%) felt it was urgent to know who would pay for the cleanup.

Based on the items that 75% or more rated important and urgent, a typical first–day breaking story about an environmental emergency situation is likely to include the following information: the company address; the name of the chemical, its use and its physical characteristics (solid, liquid, or gas; could it explode or catch on fire; etc.); its overall impact on humans; whether it could cause acute effects such as eye irritation; whether it was near a drinking water supply or other waterway; whether it could migrate from the site, and, if so, how; whether it could increase the likelihood of cancer; how much of the chemical is harmful; whether it was near hospitals, schools or other high–density institutions or highways or airports; what the permissible levels were for the chemical in the workplace or environment; and what municipal government had jurisdiction over the site. Clearly, the emphasis for the breaking story is on the basic facts concerning immediate human health effects.

Not included in the story but rated important and urgent were telephone numbers (day and night). Also rated important and urgent by reporters were the precautions they should take on–site. Interestingly, several of the reporters wrote on the survey form that they had never thought about taking precautions for their personal safety before.

Rated important but not urgent by reporters—items that reporters might research for a follow–up story—were most of the more subtle environmental and health effects, as well as the details about studies and scientists' opinions about the hazard.

Of course when journalists indicated on the survey that a particular piece of information was important and urgent, they were not necessarily claiming that they always use it in their breaking stories. Rather, they were expressing the view that this was a piece of information they felt they should have when writing the story. Three possibilities present themselves: (1) the reporter could have the information and use it; (2) the reporter could have the information and decide not to use it, perhaps for reasons of space; or (3) the reporter could be unable to find the information. For those interested in encouraging more background risk information in breaking stories, much depends on the distinction between (2) and (3). In particular, efforts to improve access to information are useful only to the extent that reporters are having trouble obtaining that information today.

Availability of Information

In Table 6.1, the number of journalists who are currently finding it difficult to obtain certain information is given in parentheses. The numbers are generally small. More importantly, they are larger for background information about the breaking story than for background information about risk. Eleven respondents (38%), for example, said they had trouble getting a night telephone number for the company or agency involved, and thirteen (45%) had trouble obtaining the company's accident record and lawsuit record.

Respondents did report some trouble finding a few items of risk background. Eight journalists (28%) had trouble finding what the permissible levels were for the chemical in question, and how serious a carcinogen it was. Seven (24%) reported trouble finding answers to each of the following: the results of scientific studies of carcinogenicity, whether scientists were sure about carcinogenicity, the effects on genetic mutation, and if the substance was related to birth defects. But for most of the background risk information on the survey, few journalists indicated they had any difficulty getting access to the information.

However, this research may under–estimate the difficulty of obtaining information. Because the instructions for the survey called for the double procedure of choosing a number *plus* circling the number for items that were difficult to obtain, it is possible that reporters neglected, in some cases, to circle the numbers. Therefore, it is expected that reporters are probably having more trouble getting information—particularly in light of comments they made in interviews—than these findings reflect. Also, since many of the more obscure risk items were rated as not being urgent by reporters, it is doubtful that they have spent a great deal of time *trying* to find the information.

In another portion of the survey, reporters were asked to rate the availability of experts, the quality of information, and the timeliness of response during an environmental emergency. Most reporters said that they were neutral or somewhat satisfied with all three. (Note that only twenty-six journalists responded to this portion of the survey.)

Concerning the availability of experts capable of providing background information, ten out of twenty-six respondents were neutral, nine said they were somewhat satisfied, five were somewhat dissatisfied, one was very satisfied, and one was very dissatisfied.

Some journalists had comments regarding the availability of experts. Elliot Goldberg of the *Gloucester County Times* said he was somewhat satisfied "except nights, weekends, and early mornings." Anita Susi of the Newark *Star-Ledger* said she was somewhat dissatisfied because "people are often afraid to talk 'on the record.' It takes skill and luck to find good contacts."

Quality of information was rated similarly. Ten out of twenty-six said they were neutral, ten said they were somewhat satisfied, and six were somewhat dissatisfied. No one was very satisfied or very dissatisfied.

The answers regarding timeliness of response were slightly different. Ten reporters said they were somewhat dissatisfied. Eight reporters claimed to be somewhat satisfied, five were neutral, and two were very dissatisfied. (Twenty-five reporters answered this question.) AnneMarie Cooke of the New Brunswick *Home News*, one of the reporters who were somewhat dissatisfied, added the following comment: "As a rule we need and want information faster than it is usually available."

Conference Survey

Two questions in the survey conducted at the Environmental Risk Reporting Symposium pertained to reporters' attitudes about risk information in a breaking story. The first asked respondents to specify whether background health risk information (a) is essential but easy to find, so it need not be provided by an independent source, (b) is essential and hard to find under deadline pressure, and so needs to be provided by an independent source, (c) is essential but not greatly used by reporters, who have it but prefer to focus on the event itself, or (d) is not all that important beyond the basic facts. Of the sixteen journalists who answered the question, fourteen chose (b) and the other two chose (c). This endorsement of the need for better background information in breaking stories is at odds with the interviews and the mail survey. The perceptions voiced at the Symposium may reflect the effects of the conference itself (including a keynote address by Stuart Diamond of the *New York Times* arguing the need for better risk information). Alternately, the discrepancy may reflect the particular values of the sorts of journalists who manage to make time to attend a conference on environmental risk reporting.

In the second question, respondents were asked to choose two locations for health risk information from the following: in the breaking story, in a sidebar to the breaking story, in a second–day follow–up, or in an in–depth feature. Fifteen journalists answered the question. Of the thirty possible choices (two for each respondent), twelve favored putting the risk information in the breaking story itself, eight in a sidebar to the breaking story, eight in a second–day follow–up, and two in an in–depth feature.

Simulation

A simulation exercise during the Symposium presented reporters with a hypothetical fire that could include toxic effects. A roster of seven experts were available to role–play any sources reporters wished to interview, from firefighters and Department of Environmental Protection personnel to industry and environmental spokespeople to unaffiliated toxicologists. Under deadline pressure, the reporters pursued the information they considered most important for their stories. Appendix F includes the simulation scenario and instructions.

The simulation reinforced several of the findings of the project's previous research. In particular, it illustrated that reporters want only the "five W's" and basic health information—not background health risk information—for the breaking story, and that they want the information to come from official sources first.

During the simulation of an early morning fire in a supermarket warehouse, reporters were much more concerned with finding out how the fire started, what the sprinkler system was like, whether there was an evacuation plan, and whether there might be injuries or deaths, than they were concerned with the potential health risks associated with the spread of toxic fumes into a nearby neighborhood. Even when sources prompted reporters with clues of dioxin emissions and chloracne rashes, they were more interested in finding out when the fire would be contained.

When reporters did begin asking about the chemicals that were contained in the warehouse and what risks they posed, they wanted to talk only to "official" sources, including police, fire department spokespeople, the Department of Environmental Protection, and the warehouse owner, even though the facilitator repeatedly offered local residents, environmentalists, and academics as sources. Near the end of the simulation reporters began asking about the skin rashes experienced by some of the area residents and firefighters. They were offered medical doctors, university professors, and toxicologists as sources, but they again asked to talk to official sources: a hospital spokesperson and the chief resident.

Following the question period, reporters were asked to write a lead paragraph for the fire story as it would appear in the morning edition of their newspaper. Nearly all reported the story as simply a fire story; aside from a brief reference to a possibly toxic plume, the health risk was not included in the leads. Dioxin and related skin rashes were saved for late in the stories. The environmental health risks associated with the fire if it spread to the adjacent battery and furniture factories were also not mentioned. Reporters felt that, until these buildings actually went up, they were not news. By contrast, technical sources felt that the potential health effects were so serious that the story should have stressed the plume and the fire's possible spread.

The simulation, as reporters pointed out, was a very limited exercise that did not necessarily reflect how all the reporters would cover such a story. For example, a larger paper would have several reporters covering the story: one at the site, one in the newsroom on the telephone, one interviewing the evacuees, etc. Also, the choice of sources was by majority rule, so the sources may not always have been the ones every reporter in the exercise would have chosen. Finally, since the reporters were not actually at the site, they could not see, hear, feel, or smell the possible disaster. However, given the consistency of response, this exercise probably does reflect how most reporters would cover an environmental emergency under a tight deadline, and how a reporter on one of the smaller dailies would cover such a story if he or she were doing it alone.

7

Options for Providing Environmental Risk Information to the Media

The Environmental Risk Reporting Project, seeing the need to distribute risk information to reporters in a timely fashion in a form that would be most useful to them, investigated the possibility of several options for doing so. The options were: (1) a Mobile Environmental Risk Information Team, (2) a 24-hour hotline, (3) an environmental risk "wire service," (4) an environmental library for each newsroom and training on how to use it, and (5) an environmental press kit. The mobile team and the hotline were researched more extensively, since they were the first options considered by the project and involved the largest investment.

As stated previously, the other options grew out of ideas and feedback from journalists and professionals in the field of environmental risk; in essence, while providing input about the first two options, reporters were slowly helping the project to develop the final ones.

All options considered—regardless of whether or not the project ultimately decided to recommend them—will first be described. Then their cost-effectiveness will be assessed. Finally, the support and opposition from reporters and other professionals will be examined for each option.

Description of the Options

Mobile Environmental Risk Information Team

Approximately five to ten times per year, the Mobile Environmental Risk Information Team would respond to environmental emergencies as soon as they occurred. The team would consist of one public health expert and one assistant. It would be housed in a van equipped with a telephone, an environmental reference library, and the equipment necessary to provide access to several full-text and numeric computer data bases such as Hazardline, the Chemical Information System group, and others. (Available data bases are listed in Appendix G.)

The basic function of the team would be to provide reporters with background chemical, technical, and environmental risk information, to interpret the information for reporters, and to help reporters understand the risks involved with the incident. Although the team would be an on–site independent news source primarily to serve reporters, it would also support first responders by relieving them of the burden of giving background information themselves. The team would not attempt to give "hard news" information to reporters: explaining the how and why of the particular crisis would remain the responsibility of emergency responders and regulatory personnel. The team would respond to the questions of reporters on–site as well as those questions called into the van from newsrooms.

Because of the nature of emergency situations, the team would cooperate with state police emergency response personnel to minimize confusion at the scene. Team members would be trained in first aid and CPR and would be familiar with basic hazardous emergency situation procedures.

If the van were equipped with a telecopier, the team could also transmit fact sheets or press releases directly to individual newsrooms. If the van were equipped with typewriters, terminals, and telephones for reporters' use, it could become an unofficial press center; with the cooperation of the state police, the Department of Environmental Protection, and other agencies, it might even become an official press center for all sources to use.

24–Hour Hotline

A 24–hour environmental risk hotline is designed to recognize reporters' need for constant access to expert information. The hotline would be staffed by at least one public health specialist. Support staff would include a data retrieval specialist and a clerical assistant. References available to reporters through the hotline would be an environmental library and related chemical and environmental computer data bases. Full text and numeric data bases would give immediate information; data bases providing abstracts or citations would be useful in identifying literature for a more comprehensive investigation. The staff would interpret the information for the reporters and suggest other areas of research.

It is expected that the heaviest use of this service would be during evening hours when a reporter's regular access to sources in government, industry, and academia is not possible. The hotline, therefore, would be staffed for sixteen hours a day, from 8:00 a.m. to 12:00 midnight, Monday through Friday. A professional answering service skilled in screening calls for emergencies—such as a medical service might use—would answer calls at all other times. The service would refer emergency calls to the staff. A weekend and holiday shift would be added when necessary.

A feature which could be added to enhance the usefulness of this option would be a telecopier so the hotline staff could send information directly to newsrooms. Another enhancement could merge the hotline with the Mobile Environmental Risk Information Team. In essence, the staff of the hotline would move to the van during major emergencies, going "on the road" and performing their background information function from the scene.

Wire Service

Environmental risk stories are often covered from the newsroom, especially at smaller newspapers where a few reporters are responsible for large areas of coverage. An environmental risk wire service would provide reporters with background risk information specific to a breaking story that was occurring locally or in another area of the state. The information would be telexed or telecopied directly to the newsroom of every daily newspaper in the state. Information could come in any of several forms: fact sheets or press releases to be used by the reporter; background sidebars or columns to be run as is; or camera–ready graphics to be incorporated into stories.

This service would be necessary an estimated five to twenty times per year; the actual number of transmissions would depend on the number of environmental emergencies that occur. (The term "wire service" is not meant to imply a single–use dedicated system, which would be impractical unless it were used far more frequently than twenty times a year. A multi-user telex system such as Business Wire would probably be best for implementation.)

All information would be well–documented and compiled by a public health specialist. Reporters could attribute the information directly to that person.

This option could be combined with the team or the hotline by giving those more ambitious projects telex capabilities.

Environmental Library

An environmental library for each newsroom would give reporters a wealth of environmental risk information at their fingertips. The health effects of chemical exposure, regulations, standards, precautions, cleanup methods, etc. are well known for many substances, and this information is published and periodically updated in books, manuals, and government publications.

This option would offer a six–volume library and a training seminar in how to use it for each daily newspaper. In order for the paper to receive the library, one person—a reporter, a staff librarian, an editor—would be required to attend the training seminar, assume custody of the library, and agree to train others in its use.

An annual refresher course, as well as updated manuals, would be included in this option.

Environmental Press Kit

The environmental risk press kit would consist of information relevant to typical breaking stories on the environment, as well as specialized information, a glossary of technical terms, and a list of the names and telephone numbers of experts on various environmental risk topics. It would include essays written by experts on various types of environmental emergencies and information about the background appropriate to include in a well covered story, as well as questions reporters might consider asking when covering such emergencies.

The press kit would be a portable document, perhaps a pocket directory so reporters could carry it with them. It would be updated regularly.

Cost Effectiveness of the Options

Table 7.1 summarizes the initial start–up costs and the yearly operational costs associated with each option, with estimates for best–case and worst–case yearly use. Appendix H gives the item–by–item breakdown and vendors for the equipment needed. Note that all figures given are exclusive of overhead expenses and indirect costs; expenses such as utilities, insurance, etc. would have to be added where applicable to obtain real costs.

Mobile Environmental Risk Information Team

The team will cost approximately $124,435 to set up initially and run for the first year. Well over half of this amount, $80,685, will be spent on the van and equipment. Salaries for personnel to run and support the van in the first year will be $43,750. The second year cost is considerably lower, $59,980, and reflects salary costs and ongoing costs such as maintenance and data base use.

At most, the team would be used ten times per year. At this rate, each trip will cost $12,443 the first year and $5,998 in subsequent years. Assuming

TABLE 7.1
Summary Cost of Options*

Option	Total Cost	FIRST YEAR Per use (optimistic)	Per use (worst case)	Total Cost	EACH ADDITIONAL YEAR Per use (optimistic)	Per use (worst case)
Team	$124,435.00	$497.74	$1,244.35	$59,980.00	$239.92	$599.80
Hotline	259,407.00	99.77	259.41	243,580.00	93.68	243.58
Wire Service	67,587.00	135.17	337.94	54,160.00	108.32	270.80
Library	32,000.00	23.67	64.00	12,100.00	8.95	24.20
Press Kit	36,000.00	9.00	22.50	16,750.00	4.19	10.47

* See text for discussion of per-use calculations. See Appendix H for details of cost figures.

optimistically that twenty-five reporters make use of the team, either on-site or by telephone, the cost of the service per reporter use would be $497.74 the first year and $239.92 after that. Assuming a worst-case scenario of only ten reporter uses per emergency, the cost per use would be $1,244.35 the first year and $599.80 thereafter.

24-Hour Hotline

A hotline would have the highest initial cost as well as the highest cost per year. Equipment costs and other start-up expenses total $65,657. Salaries and fringe benefits for employees on two shifts add $193,750. This brings the cost of starting up the hotline and running it in the first year to $259,407. In subsequent years the hotline would cost $243,580 per year.

Assuming optimistically that the hotline received two calls per week from each of twenty-five newspapers—2,600 calls per year—the cost of the service per reporter use would be $99.77 in the first year and $93.68 in subsequent years. A worst-case figure of 1,000 calls per year would put the cost of the hotline at $259.41 per use for the first year and $243.58 per use in following years.

Wire Service

A wire service can be set up on a relatively small equipment budget, but a higher cost for salaries. Equipment outlays and other expenses for the first year are estimated at $15,837. Salaries for the first year come to an estimated $51,750. The first-year budget for the wire service would total $67,587 and in subsequent years the figure would be $54,160.

An optimistic estimate of 500 uses per year (twenty transmissions to twenty-five newspapers) would make the per-use cost of the wire service $135.17 in the first year and $108.32 thereafter. Assuming a worst case of only 200 uses per year, the wire service would then cost $337.94 per use in the first year and $270.80 per use each year thereafter.

Environmental Library

Environmental libraries at all twenty-six New Jersey daily newspapers would have a total start-up cost of approximately $32,000, including $13,000 for books ($500 per newspaper) and $12,000 for a staff to select and buy the books and conduct a one-day training seminar. Subsequent annual costs would be $12,100.

Assuming that the library was used once per week at each of the twenty-six newspapers (1,352 uses), the cost per use for the first year would be

$23.67. Subsequent years would cost $8.95 per reporter use. Estimating conservatively at only 500 total uses per year, the twenty–six libraries would cost $64 per use in the first year and $24.20 per use each year thereafter.

Environmental Risk Press Kit

The total start–up cost for a press kit would be $36,000, including $24,000 for staff, and $12,000 for materials. Annual costs in following years would be $16,750.

At a projected use of twenty times per year for each of the 200 press kits in circulation (4,000 uses), the first-year cost would be $9.00 per reporter use. In subsequent years, given the same rate of use, the press kit would cost $4.19 per use. A worst–case estimate of only 1,600 uses per year would bring the cost of the press kit up to $22.50 per use for the first year and $10.47 per use in the following years.

Summary

Clearly, the most expensive option to start up and maintain is the hotline. Although the start–up equipment costs for the team are greater, the hotline must be staffed by professionals during its active operation to be most effective. The relatively high salaries of these professionals would be an ongoing cost that would not diminish over time. On the other hand, once the initial investment for the van and equipment has been made, its cost lowers considerably, since it does not need to be staffed unless there is an incident.

The limited use of the team, however, drives up its cost per use. The team would respond to a maximum of ten incidents per year, whereas the hotline would be available continuously, making it far more cost effective on a per-use basis than the team. Obviously, both of these options require a considerable investment to implement.

The wire service is considerably less expensive than either the team or the hotline to start up. Although its per–year cost in subsequent years is considerably lower than that of the hotline, the wire service is expected to be used less frequently than the hotline, driving its per–use cost up slightly higher than that of the hotline.

The library and the press kit represent modest investments that are comparable to each other. The per-use costs of both the library and the press kit are considerably less than of any of the other options. The press kit is expected to get more uses than the library; hence, its cost per use is the least expensive.

Support and Opposition

Mobile Environmental Risk Information Team

The most controversial of all the options was by far the Mobile Environmental Risk Information Team. Although twenty–two of the twenty–six journalists surveyed said that the team would be useful or enormously useful, comments received during interviews suggested that their support for the team was not as enthusiastic as the survey implied. The survey of reporters conducted at the Symposium, moreover, reflected extreme lack of support for the team: None of the seventeen respondents chose the team as their first choice from the five options, and only four of the seventeen made the team their second choice.

The journalists who supported the idea of the team gave two main reasons for doing so. The first was simply that they would support anything that would give them more information or additional sources or make their jobs a little easier. As Donna Kenyon of the Woodbridge *News Tribune* pointed out, "The more information available, the better." Jim Dao of the *Daily Journal* in Elizabeth said the team "would save hours of work; the more technical assistance available, the better." Pat Gilbert, reporter for the *Trenton Times*, called the team "one of the most important things that could be done. I don't have time to run all over" looking for explanations.

The second benefit of the team, according to reporters, is that it would give them an opportunity for a face–to–face interview at the scene. "One always suspects that not having the source at the scene could detract from the reporting job," commented Dao. (The advantage to having an on–site source is that there is less chance of the expert misinterpreting the incident. A reporter could possibly relay an inaccurate or incomplete version of the situation to an off–site expert, causing the expert to err in his or her response. As a result, the risk information might not be totally relevant to the emergency.) Other reporters simply prefer working face–to–face as opposed to over the telephone. Gordon Bishop of the Newark *Star-Ledger* claimed, "I deal only with direct sources, eyeball to eyeball, not indirect [sources]."

Journalists' opposition to the team ranged from doubts about its usefulness to strong feelings against it. First, interestingly, some reporters were afraid the team would cost too much, saying that a good list of phone numbers would help them just as much and cost a lot less. Judy Petsonk, reporter for the *Courier-Post* in Cherry Hill, said, "I see no service that could be provided by an on–site team that couldn't be performed less expensively by a hotline."

Some journalists claimed that the team's use would be limited because many newspapers do not send reporters to the scene; many emergencies are covered by phone from the newsroom. According to Chris Biddle of the *Burlington County Times*, reporters "get the how and why in the field," and the background information—precisely what the team would provide—is collected from the office. "Most deadline reporting is done by phone," according to AnneMarie Cooke of the New Brunswick *Home News*.

Bettina Boxal, environmental reporter for the *Record* of Bergen County, agreed that reporters do not need to be at the scene of every problem. "There's a limited amount of information you can get on-site," she said. Supervisors back in the office often know more than the field crew and are in a better position to talk about it, she added.

Many reporters were afraid that using the team would make their jobs "too easy." Phil Garber of the Morristown *Daily Record* warned, "Don't make it too easy for reporters," or they might get used to being spoon-fed. Reporters might stop double-checking facts and getting second opinions, he added.

Another complaint about the team was that it would offer the same information and the same sources to all reporters, thereby stifling creativity and ingenuity in finding sources or digging for information. Bettina Boxal, one of the most vocal opponents of the team, said "I'm not particularly interested in having every reporter covering the event wind up with the same information that I have." In addition, she called the team a "pre-packaged media event . . . that would undercut the credibility of the experts involved. I'd probably not use it just on principle," she said.

Others reasons reporters gave for opposing the team included that it would take too long to get to an emergency to be of any use to reporters, and that many districts did not have environmental emergencies so those reporters would not get to use it very much, if at all.

Various comments from reporters indicated that the team would not be helpful because they simply do not need the kind of information the team would dispense for their breaking stories. William Terdoslavich of the *North Jersey Advance* said that for the breaking story "you mostly want to know what happened," and that the environmental information can be included in the next-day follow-up. Bob Larkins of the *Jersey Journal* agreed, saying that he did not think the "real technical" details were needed for the breaking story. Evaluative information, such as whether the chemical was within EPA standards, would be more appropriate, he said, adding that he did not have any real problems getting this information. Wilson Barto of *The Trentonian* said that what reporters need at the scene is an evaluation of the accident, which the team would not provide.

Emergency responders and government officials also questioned the usefulness of the team. They contended that all the background information a reporter needs is already available on–site. "Every emergency response unit has the information at its fingertips,"commented Robert Ferraiuolo of the Hudson County Regional Health Commission. "Why confuse the issue with new sources?"

While it is true that emergency scenes are literally crawling with experts, they are often too busy handling the emergency—or do not see it as their role—to talk to reporters. As Jim Dao pointed out, "Though some local environmental response teams have become very adept at responding to a reporter's questions, many are uninformed or reticent about providing background on chemicals, companies, and laws."

A valid concern expressed by several emergency responders was that the team would add to the confusion at the scene. Frank Marshall, coordinator of emergency response for the New Jersey Department of Health, had reservations about adding more people to the scene. "So many people are already involved," he said. "Emergency situations are frustrating. There's no place to meet and lots of noise." Putting more players in the game, according to Marshall, could interfere with emergency procedures and add to safety concerns. "It would just be another van I'd have to warn when the wind shifted," he said.

Jim Staples, DEP's top public information officer, agreed. "Everybody—cops, ambulance people, firemen—is running around, trying to figure out which end is up and what we do first," he explained. "Nobody at that place or time has the capability to stop and deal with the media." This included, according to Staples, not having the time to keep the team informed about what was going on. "The person [team] who mans the van is going to be as out of touch with reality as the media people he's trying to help," claimed Staples.

Another disadvantage of the team is that, in time of crisis, there simply is not very much information available. If a chemical's identity and concentration in the water or air are unknown, the team would not be able to supply background information. According to Tom DiPiazza of the Hudson County *Dispatch*, "the problem is [finding out] what's there, not finding someone to talk to." Public health officials agreed that this is a basic problem at the site of an emergency. Lester Jargowsky of the Monmouth County Health Department said that in the confusion of identifying and controlling the emergency, no one has any answers, "but that's when the media is on my back."

Even when the information is available, it is often so sketchy that the associated risks are not known. This is especially true in a chemical fire when it is unclear which, or how many, chemicals are involved. "Reporters would love it if I could quantify the risk," said Ferraiuolo, adding that it is often not possible to do so.

Representatives of the chemical industry also opposed the team. Incidents that occur on company property or that involve company products should be handled by company personnel, according to Joe Caporossi, manager of health, safety, and emergency response for American Cyanamid. Craig Skaggs, public affairs manager for DuPont Chemicals, agreed. "It's not going to serve the public to have reporters talk to an M.D. or a Ph.D.," he said, adding that plant managers are already experts, that "they know more than doctors about the chemicals in their plants."

Not all emergency responders felt the team would be detrimental, however. EPA's Mike Polito said the team "wouldn't add more confusion to the scene of the accident if it's going to provide assistance [and] a place to gather and exchange ideas." Fred Rubel, also of EPA, said it might be useful to have help dealing with the press, especially if the other problems could be worked out.

24-Hour Hotline

The hotline had many more supporters than the team. In the Symposium survey, the hotline received eleven first choices and four second choices (out of seventeen), making it the most popular of the four options offered at that time. Journalists seemed to feel that it would be more useful because it would be more accessible to them and the way they most often work; by phone. William Terdoslavich said that in his district "the environmental stories tend to be drawn out. . . ." What is really needed, he said, "is a reliable contact we could reach when the government offices are closed."

Chris Biddle said the hotline "would have a greater value [than the team] for getting background information from the office." Other reporters also said they would appreciate a source they could call from the newsroom. Larry Hackett of the Newark *Star–Ledger* said, "Once your lead is together, or somebody back at the office is free, a phone call would allow for more and better questions" than an on–site source.

A hotline would not be limited to giving information to reporters only at times of emergencies. "A lot of environmental stories are based on complaints by officials and residents," explained Michael Taylor of the *Asbury Park Press*. These stories "are not breaking news disasters, yet the same information is often needed," he said. "A telephone hotline would be most useful, both for breaking news and investigative pieces."

Emergency responders favored the hotline over the team because it would help reporters and keep them off the site. Richard Kozub of the Middlesex County Health Department said that the hotline would fill the information gap for reporters. "When we give information out to reporters," he explained, "we tell them that X caused Y, and that's why we did Z.

Then reporters ask a bunch of questions about the related consequences and we say 'sorry, we don't have time to go into that right now.'"

Although a hotline may be an excellent idea, it is not an original one. There are already hotlines that exist to answer questions about chemicals and environmental risk. The most popular one with reporters is the Media Resource Service run by the Scientists' Institute for Public Information (SIPI). SIPI offers a hotline that is tied into a computer data base of experts who have agreed in advance to answer reporters' questions. The staff of SIPI can put journalists in touch with the appropriate experts in various scientific fields. There are other hotlines, such as CHEMTREC, the Chemical Transportation Emergency Center, which respond twenty–four hours a day to chemical emergencies throughout the country. Although this line is not intended for use by reporters, reporters have said that they occasionally tap into it and are not turned away. (In January 1986 the Chemical Manufacturers Association inaugurated the Chemical Referral Center, a sister hotline to CHEMTREC designed for the media and the general public.) Unlike SIPI, CHEMTREC provides the information itself, rather than the names of experts.

In addition to hotlines, various information lines are springing up, sponsored by groups such as the Natural Resources Defense Council, that reporters and citizens can call with questions and get an answer within a day or so by phone or mail. In New Jersey, the Environmental and Occupational Health Information Program at the University of Medicine and Dentistry of New Jersey—Robert Wood Johnson Medical School runs a telephone "Infoline." These lines are not equipped to deal with emergencies, but can respond relatively quickly. Lines such as these would be especially useful to reporters for follow–up or investigative articles. One of the characteristics of all hotlines, in fact, is that reporters can use them when they judge that time permits a search for background information.

Wire Service and Environmental Library

The environmental risk wire service and library were developed after much of the research had been completed. As a result, fewer reporters were questioned about these options.

In the conference survey, the wire service received almost no support, getting two first–choice votes and one second–choice vote (out of seventeen) among the four options presented. Reporters said they do not want press releases and packaged information sent to the office. They said it might never even reach the reporter working on the story, and might not be what the reporter needed. If the information was unclear or incomplete, the reporter would still have to call an expert for explanation.

The library received stronger support in the conference survey. Of the seventeen reporters who responded, four chose the library first and eight chose it second, making it second only to the hotline and far more popular than the team or the wire service. Many reporters suggested this option on their own. They claimed that newsrooms often lack even a chemical dictionary. However, they did not feel that they were qualified to choose these reference books and said they would welcome help.

Reporters also discussed some of their reservations about the library at the Symposium. There was a general concern that using the books would be difficult, that they would not be able to find the right page, or would not understand the book, or would apply the information incorrectly once they had it. Other reporters said that they disliked looking up data, that they preferred to talk to a person who could just tell them what they wanted to know. Other concerns revolved around needing quotable sources; many felt a book was inappropriate for a quotation in a newspaper article.

Most of these concerns could be remedied with the proper training of reporters in the use of the library. The library is not intended to be a substitute for interviewing experts, but rather a reference when experts are not available. The library would require space in the newsroom to house it as well as use it, since many reporters do not have their own desks.

Environmental Risk Press Kit

The idea of a press kit came too late in the project to solicit much feedback from reporters. However, many of the comments reporters made as they were talking about the other options—and environmental risk reporting in general—led the project to believe that they would use the service often enough to justify the low cost of creating it.

First, the press kit would contain a list of phone numbers of experts who could be reached during the day and, if possible, during the evening hours. Reporters repeatedly asked for "a good list of phone numbers."

Next, the press kit would contain a glossary that would provide a ready reference—and cross reference—of scientific terms that reporters could refer to when trying to decode an explanation given to them by an expert. Judy Petsonk said that she is building her own personal library on toxic substances and that pamphlets on toxins would be extremely helpful to her. Though far less complete than an environmental library, the press kit has some of the same advantages.

The press kit would also be portable—and durable—enough for the reporter to carry along in the field or move around the newsroom. Also, reporters are familiar with the use of press kits.

Finally, the press kit would contain essays or briefings by experts that would explain various angles of specific environmental breaking stories (e.g. cancer clusters, siting controversies, spills, occupational exposures, etc.), especially the pitfalls of covering each particular type of incident. As a result of these explanations, reporters would be better equipped to ask the appropriate questions in an environmental risk situation.

8

Meeting the Information Needs
of Reporters

The overall impression that can be gained from the Phase Two research—from the interviews with journalists and non–journalists, from
the mail survey, and from the conference simulation—is that reporters do
not perceive as great a need for background risk information in breaking
stories as does the project. By and large, when reporters are faced with an
environmental emergency to cover, their first priority will be to cover the
breaking story along with the very basic risk information—for example,
the immediate threat to human beings in the vicinity of the incident.

One of the assumptions at the start of this research was that reporters
were not including risk information in their articles about environmental
situations because they were having trouble gaining access to it. This is
partially true. In the mail survey, reporters identified areas in which they
had trouble finding information, such as whether a chemical increases the
likelihood of birth defects or genetic mutation, how serious a carcinogen
the chemical is, what impact the chemical has on human health, whether
the chemical increases the likelihood of cancer, etc. In interviews with
reporters, moreover, many complained that it was extremely difficult to get
sources when they needed them, especially at night and on weekends.

Both the mail survey and the simulation exercise, however, illustrated
that lack of access was not the only reason reporters were not including risk
information in their environmental articles. In the mail survey, reporters
for the most part chose basic information as important and urgent for their
first–day breaking stories. Although they considered toxicological effects,
studies, and more detailed risk data important, they did not rate them as
being urgent enough to include in first–day articles. The simulation showed
a similar trend. Reporters asked mostly physical details about the fire and
the warehouse. Although they asked some questions about risk late in the

exercise, the answers to those questions would have appeared late in their stories, if at all.

To put it another way, reporters view environmental risk as an angle of the story rather than the story itself. Especially when the "news" aspect of an environmental incident is dramatic—leaping flames, clouds of vapor, ducks covered with oil—reporters are not likely to look very far for background information about risk.

This does not mean that journalists necessarily view environmental risk information as insignificant. Most journalists are dedicated to reporting all issues as thoroughly as they can and take pride in the fact that they are, by and large, successful in communicating urgent and important news to the public. Still, it is abundantly clear that many of the journalists sampled have a fundamentally different view than the non–journalists interviewed and the project researchers regarding the degree of need for risk information in environmental news stories. In the judgment of the authors, based on the research reported in Phase One, background environmental risk information is not getting as much coverage as it should—in even the "best" environmental stories—to fully inform the public of risks to which it may be exposed. The problem is especially serious, moreover, with respect to breaking environmental stories such as fires and spills—the stories likely to attract the largest audience. These are judgments with which the journalists interviewed in Phase Two would not necessarily agree.

Given the above, simply improving reporters' access to risk information may not, in itself, yield substantial improvements in background risk coverage. Just as important as access to information is an educational program aimed at helping reporters understand and interpret the risk information they have. An important component of such an educational program, moreover, is a dialogue between journalists and technical experts over how much and what sort of background risk information belongs in a breaking news story. Journalistic standards of newsworthiness do respond to such educational efforts; the increasing sophistication of coverage of public opinion polls is a case in point.

A sound assessment of the five options covered in this research must therefore consider not only cost and feasibility in improving access to risk information, but also educational impact on journalists' views on the newsworthiness of environmental risk information.

The Mobile Environmental Risk Information Team is very expensive. As pointed out in the costs section, it is the most expensive option on a per–use basis because it would be used no more than ten times per year. Although it would make risk information available at the scene, there is no guarantee that the basic information—the chemical in question, etc.—

would be available from emergency responders in a time frame that would make the information the team could supply meaningful. In short, if the chemical had not been identified, the team could not supply background information on it.

Although the team received initial support from reporters, it was largely for reasons of convenience; most reporters said that they would welcome *any* additional information, no matter what form it took. They could not guarantee they would use it, but they wanted as much information as they could get. Obviously, the team is too large an investment to be used in this manner.

An overwhelming drawback of the team was that emergency responders were almost unanimously against it, saying that it would be in the way, that there was already too much confusion at the scene of an incident, and that emergency response groups themselves were quite capable of handling the press. Industry people were against anyone outside of their own companies speaking to the press about incidents that concerned them.

The team would not contribute greatly to reporters' education either, since it would primarily be responding to an immediate need for information that could be rushed back to the newsroom, included (or not included) in a story written under deadline pressure, and then forgotten.

The 24–hour hotline, the most expensive of the options, would fulfill some of the requirements for reporters' needs more adequately than the team. Reporters repeatedly asked for telephone numbers, or a place where they could get information when their usual contacts were unavailable. Since many reporters work almost exclusively by telephone—especially on the smaller papers where a few reporters must cover several stories at once—a hotline would be much more convenient than the team. Reporters also prefer a source of background information for non–emergency background stories, a need the hotline could meet and the team could not.

However, because the hotline is such an expensive proposition, it would have to be used extremely frequently to make it cost–effective. Since other phone lines (24–hour hotlines as well as "information lines") are springing up all over the country, including the very effective one operated by SIPI, the use that this particular hotline would get probably would not justify its high cost.

The hotline would probably have more educational value for reporters than the team because reporters could call about any question on risk, at any time, even if they were not working under a specific story deadline. Again, this does not present a large enough gain to justify the expense.

The wire service, which was uniformly panned by reporters, has a relatively low price tag, but the use it would get and the reporters it would inform would be negligible. This option simply does not fit reporters' ideas of how they want to cover stories, and, according to reporters, would not give them a quotable source.

Of all the options, the ones that come closest to filling the needs of reporters, as well as being relatively low–cost and easily implemented, are the environmental library and the environmental risk press kit.

The library was recommended by several reporters at the Environmental Risk Reporting Symposium in October 1985. Reporters cited the need for references available to them in the newsroom that they could turn to at any time. Reporters' main concerns about the library were that they would have difficulty using it, and that they would still need a quotable source.

Of course, the library would be no substitute for an interview with an expert. It would serve as a reference that would supplement facts the reporter already had. In addition, reporters who were trained by the Environmental Risk Reporting Project (who subsequently returned to their papers and trained other reporters) would have a better grasp of the kind of information available to include in stories. Hence, the library would also fill to some extent the need for educating reporters about risk.

Additionally, the library would be relatively inexpensive to implement.

The environmental risk press kit is the least expensive of the options and seems to fill the needs identified by many reporters interviewed during this research. The request for day and night telephone numbers for experts and other sources, which the press kit would supply, was heard repeatedly. Another request reporters had was for something that would help them explain risk issues "in layman's terms to the reader," according to Chris Biddle, reporter for the *Burlington County Times*. John Hudzinski of the *Asbury Park Press*, among others, also cited that need, using as an example a handbook of thumbnail descriptions that the New Jersey Natural Gas Company had handed out.

The press kit is intended to provide just this kind of help to reporters. As well as supplying telephone numbers, it would include short essays written by experts that would discuss the important things to look for in a particular environmental incident, thereby helping reporters to do a better job of covering environmental risk issues. A glossary of technical terms would promote use of risk details that reporters might not currently use because they do not know how to explain them to their readers. The press kit would be portable and in a form reporters were used to; thus, they would be more likely to use it than the more cumbersome options. Finally, the press kit responds to the need for education as well as access, by giving reporters the tools to understand the importance of risk information in an environmental story.

It should be pointed out that the Phase Two research reinforced the value of another "option": continuing education for reporters and editors. As stated by Anne Morris, executive director of the Association of New Jersey Environmental Commissions, there are a "handful of underlying issues" that could be identified and taught to journalists. "Once a reporter . . . has a handle on three or five of these issues, the others come easier," she added. Her suggestion that the Environmental Risk Reporting Project "run a series of workshops on basic principles . . . a tutorial in the kind of background they [reporters] need . . . so when they go to an event they are already looking at the event in . . . context," is well taken and reflects the overall conclusions of this project.

9

Summary and Conclusions

The Environmental Risk Reporting Project developed out of a need perceived by government, scientists, and some journalists to improve the reporting of environmental risk to the public. Every state in the nation faces environmental hazards, and informed publics are necessary for the management of environmental risk. Nowhere is this more true than in New Jersey, and so it was most useful to explore New Jersey's "best" environmental news coverage, and strategies for improving it.

Phase One

The first goal of the Environmental Risk Reporting Project was to explore the strengths and weaknesses of environmental risk reporting by using New Jersey's best environmental risk stories as a case study. The articles analyzed were chosen by the editors of the twenty–six daily newspapers in New Jersey as representing the best articles published in 1984 on the subject. The collection of articles—the archive—consists of 248 articles which contain 6,486 paragraphs.

The analysis of the archive took two forms, a formal content analysis and a more subjective expert analysis. The formal content analysis focused on two characteristics of the archive: (1) Source—that is, where the information in the newspaper article came from; and (2) Risk—that is, what the newspaper article stated about the presence of a hazardous substance, or about the degree of risk arising from an environmental situation. Data were collected on two units of analysis: the article as a whole and each individual paragraph. In all, there were thirteen categories of sources— federal government, state government, county government, local government, general government, industry, workers, advocacy groups, citizens, experts, unattributed, mixed attribution, and other. There were seven categories of risk—risky, not risky, mixed opinion if risky, substance present, not present, mixed opinion if present, and no mention of risk.

For the subjective analysis, four experts—an environmental activist, a scientist, a journalist, and an industry representative—spent an intensive weekend reading and analyzing various aspects of the archive including treatment of risk, tone, bias, accuracy, clarity, enterprise, newsworthiness, and individual differences. The experts' analysis of the archive supplied insight and depth to trends discovered in the formal content analysis.

The most significant findings, supported by both the formal analysis and the expert analysis, follow:

1. There exists a paucity of information about environmental risk in the archive. While the experts recognized that reporters' deadline pressures and inaccessibility of information were partly responsible, they also felt that many reporters and editors are not sufficiently sensitive to or interested in the subject of environmental risk to include it in articles about environmental issues. The experts also found that reporters seemed more comfortable reporting environmental politics than environmental risk.

2. When environmental risk is reported in the archive, it is more alarming than reassuring. Although three of the four experts felt that the archive portrayed a far more alarming picture of the state's environmental issues than is justified by reality, the project did not measure quantitatively if the news stories differed from reality—because of the difficulty of determining what reality is.

3. Risk information in the archive comes largely from government, industry, and unattributed sources. Reporters do not greatly rely on uninvolved experts for information about risk.

4. Reporting of environmental risk tends toward the extremes (a situation is risky or not risky, a substance is present or not present) rather than quoting sources who take an intermediate or tentative position.

5. Bias (a major concern voiced during the expert analysis), when it occurs, is a product of a reporter relying too heavily on a particular source in a particular article, rather than his or her intentional bias. A biased tone can also occur when reporters try to translate technical jargon into more familiar—but often more volatile—lay terms. However, it is important to note that articles were generally accurate, and that inaccuracies were more in the realm of missing information or context rather than errors of fact. The flagrant distortions or "lies" about which sources sometimes complain are simply not a characteristic of the archive.

Recommendations for Reporters and Editors

The study of New Jersey's best press coverage of environmental risk yielded a number of insights about the strengths and weaknesses of environmental risk reporting. The formal content analysis provided a necessary baseline for comparison, and the expert analysis provided understanding about the importance of conveying certain types of risk information to the public. The project's assessment of the gap between what is reported and what should be reported is the basis for the following recommendations made to the journalistic profession. Developing the necessary support materials for incorporating these recommendations into daily environmental risk reporting is one of the goals of the Environmental Risk Reporting Project.

1. Reporters and editors should recognize that environmental risk is an important technical story as well as an important political story, and should try not to subordinate the former to the latter. In stories about environmental controversies, risk information should be more plentiful than it is.

2. Reporters should avoid treating environmental risk as a dichotomy that either "is" or "is not." The important questions for public understanding and public policy are how much risk, under what circumstances, and with what degree of certainty. Reporters should learn how to find sources who can answer these questions, how to understand the answers, and how to convey these answers clearly and interestingly to readers.

3. A standard paragraph or two should be inserted into articles about environmental risk that would include necessary information but be succinct enough not to pre–empt the "news" thrust of the story. According to the panel of experts, the minimum basic risk information in a hard news story involving a toxic substance should include: (1) how much of the substance was detected, (2) the legal standard (if any) for the substance, and who determined that standard, (3) the health risk (e.g. lung cancer) the standard is based on, and (4) the extent of debate over whether the standard is too stringent or not stringent enough.

4. Newspapers should use more graphics and other visual aids to illustrate points about environmental risk.

5. Less scientific jargon should be used by reporters, but reporters should be careful when translating jargon into more familiar terms that they do so accurately and without sensationalism. As a necessary prerequisite, reporters should make sure they understand the technical material they plan to explain.

6. Risk information should not be buried at the end of a long series or in special sections or sidebars that few people read under normal circumstances. It is important to put some relevant risk information in the first few paragraphs of hard news articles.

7. Reporters should ask more questions of environmental risk experts and do more follow–up on stories about environmental risk.

8. Newspapers should consider hiring specialized environmental reporters who are as comfortable with the science as with the politics in the story. General assignment reporters who do not have a background in environmental matters should be trained to have a greater knowledge of and sensitivity to the subject they are covering. Wherever possible, continuing environmental stories should be covered by the same reporter—whether an environmental specialist or not—to provide continuity and necessary background.

9. Editors should be trained regarding the key problems of an environmental risk story so they can recognize them when editing news copy and adjust the story accordingly.

10. Reporters and editors should note that the norms of journalism practice lead them to pay more attention to alarming risk information than to reassuring risk information. While danger is genuinely more newsworthy than safety, and truth is not always in the middle, reporters and editors should try to prevent their articles on environmental risk from stressing the alarming side more than available information justifies.

11. Reporters, editors, and headline writers should be more sensitive to the possibility of misleading impressions given to the public by sensational headlines and oversimplified leads to environmental risk stories. In particular, headlines and leads should not baldly assert risk when the rest of the story shows that the degree of risk is in dispute.

12. Reporters and editors should concentrate more of their effort on finding and using sources whose positions on environmental risk are intermediate, mixed, or tentative. When sources express views that are intermediate, reporters should be careful not to remove the qualifiers; efforts to simplify and clarify the point risk distorting it in the direction of more extremeness or more certainty than the situation justifies. Journalists should understand that the middle is as much a position as the extremes, and it is a position that readers need to know exists.

13. Reporters and editors should become more aware of individual stances taken by government, industry, citizens, and other sources on environmental risk issues in order to balance their sources in an article. An industry spokesperson or an environmental activist, for example, should not normally be relied on as the sole source for an article on environmental risk. In general, reporters should seek out more sources—with varied opinions—for environmental risk articles.

14. Reporters should include a short synopsis of events to date in articles covering an ongoing environmental risk controversy, rather than assume all readers have followed the story.

15. Reporters should try to include more detail in their articles on environmental risk, including the results of controlled scientific studies and other evidence. Sources who support their opinions with hard evidence are worth distinguishing from sources who offer only opin-

ions, though both deserve to be covered. The tentativeness and uncertainty of much research on environmental risk should also be noted, but should not be used as a justification for treating risk as purely a matter of opinion.

16. Reporters should seek out expert sources who are comparatively uninvolved in a particular environmental controversy, and should rely more on such sources for their background information on risk. To assure the availability of expert sources under hard news deadline pressure, reporters should establish relationships in advance with local toxicologists, epidemiologists, waste engineers, and other experts.

17. Reporters should continue to pay particular attention to accuracy when conveying technical information, recognizing that the complexity and unfamiliarity of the content make accuracy difficult to achieve, especially as reporters work to include more technical detail in their stories. When in doubt, reporters should check on the accuracy of their technical information with their expert sources.

Phase Two

Based on the findings of Phase One, two main goals were developed for Phase Two of the project. The first goal was to identify the reasons why more environmental risk information is not getting into news stories about hazardous substances, especially first–day breaking stories. Based on the project's conviction that environmental risk information should become a more intrinsic component of news articles, the second goal was to evaluate a series of options for providing environmental risk information to reporters and, thereby, to the public.

Attitudes toward Environmental Risk Information

Several different methods were used to determine the attitudes of reporters toward environmental risk information. First, telephone interviews were conducted with reporters at each of the twenty–six New Jersey daily newspapers. These reporters were chosen based on their authorship of articles in the archive collected during Phase One of the project or referrals made by editors. Telephone interviews were followed by an in–depth mail survey (Appendix D) with the same respondents. These data were supplemented by a participant survey distributed at the project's Environmental Risk Reporting Symposium conducted on October 4, 1985 at the University of Medicine and Dentistry of New Jersey—Robert Wood Johnson Medical School in Piscataway, New Jersey. Interviews were also conducted with industry representatives, local health officers, emergency response personnel, environmental activists, academic scientists, and government officials. The significant findings of these interviews and surveys follow.

1. Reporters do not perceive a great need for background risk information in breaking stories about hazardous environmental situations. When reporters are faced with an environmental emergency, their first priority is to cover the breaking story itself—the fire story, the leak story, etc.
2. When reporters do include risk information in breaking stories, it is the most basic risk information, that is, the immediate threat to human health.
3. In some cases, reporters have trouble finding risk information, but, in general, the little they want in their breaking stories they have little trouble finding. Reporters' main complaint about access to information pertained to results of tests that were not available in time for the first-day story.
4. When reporters do want risk information, they want it chiefly from official—preferably government—sources.

The Environmental Risk Reporting Project concluded that education is at least as important as access for improving risk reporting, and that in order to encourage reporters to be more interested in putting risk information into their stories, it is crucial to engage in an ongoing educational dialogue about the importance of background risk information in environmental journalism. This type of dialogue can easily be incorporated into special workshops and seminars sponsored by the various professional organizations in journalism and in–house training sessions at individual newspapers.

The Environmental Risk Reporting Project has conducted just such seminars and training sessions for the New Jersey Professional Chapter and the Region One Conference of the Society of Professional Journalists, Sigma Delta Chi; for the New Jersey Press Association; and for *The Record* of Hackensack, New Jersey. It has also produced a one–hour videotape, "Covering An Environmental Accident," for distribution to journalism schools and other institutions around the country.

Options for Providing Environmental Risk Information to Journalists

The second goal was to investigate the feasibility of various devices for getting environmental risk information to reporters and, hence, into their newspapers. Among the options evaluated were: (1) a Mobile Environmental Risk Information Team that would travel to the scene of an environmental emergency and give background information to reporters; (2) a 24–

hour environmental risk hotline that would staff public health experts around the clock to answer reporters' called-in questions about environmental risk; (3) a "wire service" that would telex or telecopy fact sheets, press releases, or ready-to-use background stories and graphics on environmental risk situations directly to newsrooms; (4) an environmental risk library of relevant reference books for each newsroom, with training on how to use them for at least one reporter per newsroom; and (5) an environmental risk press kit that would include names and telephone numbers of experts from different fields, a glossary of technical terms, and short essays or briefings by experts on strategies for covering particular types of environmental risk situations.

The project's evaluations are based on interviews and surveys with journalists, interviews with industry representatives, local health officials, emergency response personnel, environmental activists, academic scientists, and government officials, as well as a cost analysis of each option that determined the initial investment and yearly expense. Based on these evaluations, the project offers the following conclusions:

1. A Mobile Environmental Risk Information Team would be extremely costly to start up, with major expenditures for equipment and transportation. Although these costs would diminish in subsequent years, the use of the team would be limited—ten times per year at the most—so, the per-use cost of this option is very high. In addition, the idea of the team was not popular with journalists and was very unpopular with emergency responders and industry representatives. The team also fails to fulfill the education standard for an effective approach to the problem; that is, it would not encourage dialogue about how to cover risk. For these reasons the project concludes that a Mobile Environmental Risk Information Team is not a feasible option for delivering environmental risk information to journalists.

2. The hotline was the most expensive option considered, because it would employ qualified health experts around the clock to answer reporters' questions. The large expense for salaries would not diminish over time. The hotline satisfies the education standard better than the mobile team, in that reporters could call any time, not just when they were covering an emergency. The hotline was also relatively popular with reporters. Hotlines are, in fact, extremely useful in many fields for many purposes. They are expensive if their personnel are paid, but their expense is often justified in terms of cost per call. Fortunately, there are already hotlines that exist to answer questions about chemicals and environmental risk, and more are planned. The existence and promise of other hotlines (both regional and nationwide), would cause this new New Jersey based hotline for journalists to be underused, and therefore infeasible and unnecessary.

3. The wire service, which received almost no support from reporters, had a relatively low price tag, but the use it would get and the reporters it would inform would be negligible. This option simply did not fit reporters' ideas of how they wanted to cover stories.

4. The environmental risk library would be relatively inexpensive to implement, and was well received by reporters. Many asked for such a service on their own, in fact. Since it would be a readily available reference, it would partially meet the need to educate reporters about risk, although it would be no substitute for interviewing experts. It would be useful for both environmental emergencies and chronic environmental risk situations. The newsroom library, combined with mandatory training and annual refresher courses, is one option that should be taken seriously by any group wishing to enhance the availability of environmental risk information to the public.

5. The environmental risk press kit was the least expensive of the options. Although the idea for the press kit was developed too late in the project to solicit much feedback about it from reporters, it nonetheless responds to many of the desires reporters expressed—for example, the need for telephone numbers of experts and briefings on various environmental situations. By giving reporters the tools to understand an incident and put it into context, the press kit would also satisfy the need to educate journalists.

Recommendations for Providing Risk Information to the Media

Four central recommendations emerge from the findings reported above:

1. The concepts of a Mobile Environmental Risk Information Team and an environmental risk wire service should be abandoned, and while the concept of an environmental risk hotline is a good one, additional hotlines are probably not needed in most states.

2. Funding should be sought for a program to provide environmental risk libraries for the offices of newspapers and broadcast stations.

3. An environmental risk press kit should be designed, tested, and distributed nationally.

4. Continuing education programs on environmental risk for reporters and editors should be offered throughout the country.

The Environmental Risk Reporting Project has already begun to implement the third recommendation, and has an ongoing program to implement the fourth. A prototype environmental risk press kit is scheduled for testing in 1988–89, in preparation for national distribution. The project's continuing education program includes a videotape on "Covering An Environmental Accident" and a series of workshops and role–playing training sessions for reporters, editors, and environmental risk news sources.

Improving the availability of environmental risk information to the media, and thus the reporting of environmental risk to the public, is critical for the management of environmental problems. Journalists must be provided not only with the environmental risk information they need to adequately inform the public, but also with the opportunity to enhance their appreciation of the importance of "risk" as an issue in environmental news coverage.

Appendix A:
Content Analysis Coding Instructions and Coding Sheet

Content Analysis Instructions

This is a content analysis of newspaper articles submitted by editors as examples of how they cover environmental risk. In this stage of the analysis, we are focusing on only two questions: the sources of the articles and their approach to the risk issue. You will be looking separately at each paragraph in the article, and for each paragraph you will be checking two boxes—one box for the source of that paragraph, and one box for the paragraph's approach to risk.

Preliminary Matters

1. Read the article to get a general sense of its meaning.
2. Number the paragraphs in the article. You can do this right on your copy. Count as a paragraph every indent, including bullets, even if it is not a complete sentence.
3. Fill out the information on the left edge of the coding sheet—newspaper, headline, date, etc.

Sources

The source of a paragraph is the newsmaker to whom that paragraph is attributed. That is, the source is the person who "said" or "acknowledged" or "claimed" etc. the information in the paragraph. This is true regardless of whether the paragraph is quotation or paraphrase. If the paragraph has no attribution (for example, straight narration of what the reporter saw happening) it will be coded as Unattributed. However, if a paragraph continues a quotation or paraphrase from the preceding paragraph, assume continuing attribution. In other words, you are trying to determine *who gave the reporter* the information in the paragraph.

Note that the source need not be named. "Federal officials said . . ." would be coded as Federal Government; "EPA inspector Mary Jones said" would also be coded as Federal Government. If it is clear that the paragraph reports what a source said, code for that source even if there is no "said" or equivalent. For example, "Federal officials were concerned yesterday that the spill might explode." But "EPA Inspector Mary Jones shut down the plant" is Unattributed.

You are interested in the reporter's source, even if that source got the information from other sources. "The mayor said that state officials told her that . . ." would be coded as Local Government (for the mayor), *not* State Government.

You may use all information in the story to determine the source of the paragraph. An early paragraph may identify George Smith as an industry spokesman. Later paragraphs quoting or paraphrasing Smith would of course be coded as Industry. The same is true backwards (though this is much less common). In a feature story, for example, the first paragraph may quote John Doe about his concerns over toxic dumping, and then the second paragraph may identify Doe as the county health officer. Code the first paragraph as County Government in this case.

If the source is a document, code it for the *document's* source. Union records would be coded as Workers & Unions; state regulations would be coded as State Government.

- *Federal government:* Environmental Protection Agency (EPA) other federal agencies; members of Congress; etc.
- *State government:* Department of Environmental Protection (DEP) other state agencies; state legislators; etc.
- *County government:* County health officers, sheriff's officers; freeholders; other county officials; etc.
- *Local government:* Police (unless state police); firefighters; municipal health officers; mayor; other local officials; etc.
- *Government general:* Broad references to government ("officials," "inspectors," "authorities," etc.); mixtures of government levels ("federal and state health inspectors," etc.).
- *Industry and industry associations:* Company officials; company spokespeople; plant managers; Chemical Manufacturers Association; Business and Industry Council; etc.
- *Workers and unions:* Individual workers; union officials; union spokespeople; strikers; etc.
- *Advocacy/environmental/citizens' groups:* Local, state, or national organizations concerned with environmental risk issues or specific local controversies; Sierra Club; New Jersey Environmental Lobby; Public Interest Research Group; etc.
- *Citizens/bystanders/individuals:* Residents; neighbors; passers–by; witnesses; individuals not connected to the event/story in any institutional role; etc.

- *Experts:* Experts (at a university, a hospital, etc.) contacted by the reporter for background or technical information. Do not include experts provided by newsmakers, such as government agencies or industry or citizens' groups. Do include general "experts believe" kinds of statements.
- *Unattributed:* No source—e.g., "Toxic wastes are likely to be the issue of the eighties"; "Firefighters arrived at 6 a.m."; etc.
- *Mixed attribution:* Several sources not in the same coding category— e.g., "While industry sources said . . . DEP officials maintained. . . ."
- *Other:* Uncodable in the above categories. Indicate the source in the space provided.

Risk

Once you have identified the source of the paragraph, consider the paragraph's approach to the issue of risk. The key question you must determine is whether the paragraph focuses on the *riskiness* of a problem or on the *presence* of that problem (or neither). This will become clear in the explanation that follows.

Consider a particular substance, say dioxin. One set of risk questions has to do with how dangerous dioxin is—whether it causes cancer in animals, how large a dose can damage humans, etc. We call this *Risk*. A closely related set of questions has to do with whether dioxin is present in a particular landfill or manufacturing process or effluent. We call this *Presence*. The same distinction applies to any discussion of environmental risk: Is the focus on whether a substance (assumed or suspected to be present) is risky, or is the focus on whether a substance (assumed or suspected to be risky) is present? Consider the following two paragraphs:

> Results of samples taken by the county health department showed measurable levels of copper and volatile organic solvents, county officials said.

> The levels were considerably lower than the point at which a danger is posed to human health, according to County Health Officer John Doe.

The first paragraph concerns *Presence*, while the second paragraph focuses on *Risk*.

Sometimes the distinction is difficult to draw. "State officials expressed concern over whether the unidentified emission might include cancer-causing chemicals" doesn't clearly indicate whether the concern is Presence or Risk. Arguably it is both.

Follow this rule: If the paragraph is clearly about risk, code as Risk. If it is clearly about presence, code as Presence. If it seems to be both, code as Risk. If it is neither, code as Zilch. "Zilch" paragraphs include the actions of newsmakers, questions of legality, etc.—anything other than assessments of the riskiness/non–riskiness of a possible hazard or its presence/non–presence.

Once you have determined that a paragraph is about Risk or Presence, you must decide *which side it is on*:

- *Risk–claiming:* The paragraph asserts the existence of risk. This includes paragraphs that state an opinion that a substance is risky, or paragraphs that express a concern, or paragraphs providing evidence of riskiness. The claim *must* be explicit. Don't code a paragraph because the information it contains seems risky to you; code it only if it is clearly asserting riskiness.
- *Risk–denying:* The paragraph denies the existence of risk, or denies the risk is substantial. The paragraph may state an opinion or provide evidence. Once again, the content must be explicit. In the example above the second paragraph is risk–denying.
- *Risk—mixed/can't tell:* The paragraph deals explicitly with riskiness, but takes an intermediate position or no position or both positions on the extent of the risk. Typical examples are paragraphs that the study was inconclusive or the level was moderate, or paragraphs contrasting the positions of opposing sides, or paragraphs asserting that little is known about the health effects of the substance.
- *Presence–claiming:* The paragraph asserts the presence of the substance assumed to be risky. Include opinions that the substance is present, expressions of concern that it may be present, and evidence that it is present. In the previous example, the first paragraph is presence–claiming.
- *Presence–denying:* The paragraph denies the presence of the substance assumed to be risky. Include opinions and evidence.
- *Presence—mixed/can't tell:* The paragraph deals explicitly with presence, but takes an intermediate position or no position or both positions on the question. Typical examples are paragraphs that the authorities plan to test for the substance, or that opposing sides disagree on whether it is present.
- *Zilch:* The paragraph deals with neither risk nor presence. It may have information that you would find relevant to risk issues, but it doesn't assert the relevance. For example, a paragraph that a 1981 lawsuit found the company was not violating any environmental laws is a "zilch" paragraph.

To sum up. . . . If a paragraph assumes a substance or situation is probably risky and focuses on whether or not it is present, code Presence–claiming if it suggests the answer is Yes, code Presence–denying if it suggests No, and code Presence—mixed/can't tell if it leans neither way. If the paragraph assumes the substance or situation is probably present and focuses on whether or not it is dangerous, code Risk–claiming if it suggests the answer is Yes, code Risk–denying if it suggests the answer is No, and code Risk—mixed/can't tell if it leans neither way. If the paragraph deals equally with Risk and Presence, code it as a Risk paragraph. Finally, if the paragraph does not explicitly address the presence or the riskiness of a potential hazard, code it as Zilch.

Note that a paragraph focused on presence may mention risk in passing—e.g., "Environmentalists charged that the plant is discharging PCBs, a hazardous chemical, into the Spring River." Code this as Presence–claiming. By contrast, "Environmentalists charged that the PCBs discharged by the plant pose a long–term threat to potable water supplies along the Spring River" would be coded as Risk–claiming.

Do not reason backwards. If a paragraph late in the article contains information about risk, for example, do not let that alter your coding of the earlier paragraphs.

Treat past risk the same as present risk. In an article on a fire, for example, a paragraph asserting that there would have been a health risk if the fire had spread to a nearby chemical factory should be coded as Risk–claiming.

When in doubt, code the paragraph as Zilch. Only paragraphs that *clearly* deal with risk or presence should be coded that way.

Please be sure you have digested these instructions thoroughly before you begin!

CODING SHEET

Newspaper _____

Date _____

( ) # photos

( ) # charts/diagrams

( ) # other art

( ) Series

( ) Package

( ) Neither

PROBLEMS:

I.D. # _____

Headline _____

Byline _____

( ) Hard news

( ) Feature

( ) Background

# of Grafs _____

( ) Investigative

( ) Other (what?)

Paragraphs

	1	2	3	4	5	6	7	8	9	10	11	12	13	14	15	16
Federal government	1	1	1	1	1	1	1	1	1	1	1	1	1	1	1	1
State government	2	2	2	2	2	2	2	2	2	2	2	2	2	2	2	2
County government	3	3	3	3	3	3	3	3	3	3	3	3	3	3	3	3
Local government	4	4	4	4	4	4	4	4	4	4	4	4	4	4	4	4
Government general	5	5	5	5	5	5	5	5	5	5	5	5	5	5	5	5
Industry & industry assns.	6	6	6	6	6	6	6	6	6	6	6	6	6	6	6	6
Workers & unions	7	7	7	7	7	7	7	7	7	7	7	7	7	7	7	7
Advocacy/envl/citizens' groups	8	8	8	8	8	8	8	8	8	8	8	8	8	8	8	8
Citizens/bystanders/individuals	9	9	9	9	9	9	9	9	9	9	9	9	9	9	9	9
Experts (not involved)	10	10	10	10	10	10	10	10	10	10	10	10	10	10	10	10
Unattributed	11	11	11	11	11	11	11	11	11	11	11	11	11	11	11	11
Mixed attribution	12	12	12	12	12	12	12	12	12	12	12	12	12	12	12	12
Other List:	13	13	13	13	13	13	13	13	13	13	13	13	13	13	13	13
Claims the stuff is risky	1	1	1	1	1	1	1	1	1	1	1	1	1	1	1	1
Denies the stuff is risky	2	2	2	2	2	2	2	2	2	2	2	2	2	2	2	2
Can't tell/mixed op. if risky	3	3	3	3	3	3	3	3	3	3	3	3	3	3	3	3
Claims risky stuff is present	4	4	4	4	4	4	4	4	4	4	4	4	4	4	4	4
Denies risky stuff is present	5	5	5	5	5	5	5	5	5	5	5	5	5	5	5	5
Can't tell/mixed op. if present	6	6	6	6	6	6	6	6	6	6	6	6	6	6	6	6
Zilch	7	7	7	7	7	7	7	7	7	7	7	7	7	7	7	7

Appendix B:
Expert Analysis Schedule and Instructions

Archive Evaluation: Tentative Schedule

Friday, August 23:

2:00– 2:30	Check–in
*2:30– 3:00	"Orientation"; agreement on evaluation standards
3:00– 5:30	Packet I: Reading
*5:30– 7:00	Packet I: Discussion
7:00– 9:00	Dinner
9:00–?	Packet II: Reading

Saturday, August 24:

?– 9:00	Packet II: Reading
*9:00–10:30	Packet II: Discussion
10:30–12:30	Packet III: Reading
12:30– 2:00	Lunch
*2:00– 3:30	Packet III: Discussion
3:30– 5:30	Packet IV: Reading
*5:30– 7:00	Packet IV: Discussion
7:00– 9:00	Dinner
9:00–?	Packets V and VI: Reading

Sunday, August 25:

?–10:30	Packets V and VI: Reading
*10:30–12:00	Packets V and VI: Discussion
12:00– 1:00	Individual Overall Evaluations
1:00– 2:00	Lunch and general discussion

*These sessions will take place in the Seth Boyden Room of the Hilton Gateway in Newark. You are welcome to use the Seth Boyden room for reading, or to read on your own if you prefer.

Please note that this is a *tentative* schedule. If reading takes more or less time than we anticipate, the schedule will be adjusted accordingly.

MEMO TO: Jim Detjen
            Jim Lanard
            Eugene Murphy
            Jim Sederis
FROM: Peter Sandman
SUBJECT: Archive Evaluation
DATE: August 21, 1985

Thank you for agreeing to help us evaluate the archive we have collected of environmental risk reporting by New Jersey newspapers. We will start our weekend together by briefly talking through some possible standards for evaluating the archive. This memo will try to cover other questions you may have about what you're getting into.

1. *Who are you?* You'll meet each other and have a lot of time together over the next 48 hours, but briefly: Jim Detjen is an investigative reporter for the *Philadelphia Inquirer*, specializing in environmental and energy coverage. Jim Lanard is lobbyist for the New Jersey Environmental Lobby, and one of the most thoroughly covered environmental activists in the state. Eugene Murphy is manager of public information for Public Service Electric and Gas, where he copes with a full range of environmental stories. Jim Sederis is a chemical engineer and head of his own consulting company, involved in hazardous waste facility siting among other issues.

   Your stereotypes, then: reporter, activist, industry person, scientist. We invited each of you in part to represent your stereotype, to assess the archive from your particular point of view. But each of you was also invited in part because of your reputation for reasonableness, for negotiation, for being able to understand and respond to points of view different from your own.

2. *Who are we?* Environmental Risk Reporting is the six people listed on this stationery. We are funded by a grant from the National Science Foundation Industry/University Cooperative Center for Research in Hazardous and Toxic Substances. In addition to the archive that you will be working on this weekend, our project includes two training conferences for journalists (at one of which, October 4, you will discuss the archive) and a feasibility study of a hazardous waste emergency information response team. We have another grant from the same source to study how scientists and others can improve their communication of risk information to the media.

3. *What is the archive?* The archive is a collection of New Jersey newspaper articles on environmental risk, almost all of them from 1984. The articles were chosen by the editors of the state's 26 daily newspapers, as representative of their best work. Where the editors offered

us more articles than we could use, we simply chose the longest ones. We asked the editors to choose articles dealing with environmental risk—that is, articles raising questions of possible threats to public health or environmental quality.

Quite apart from your work this weekend, these articles are being subjected to a formal "content analysis" of measurable variables. We will know from the content analysis the length of the average article, how often it quotes government or industry or environmentalist sources, how often it quotes a source asserting or denying serious risk, etc. But a lot of what we would like to learn from the archive cannot be learned by counting. That's where you come in.

4. *What is our goal for the weekend?* We want to come out of the weekend with a list of the strengths and weaknesses of New Jersey environmental risk reporting, as demonstrated by the archive. We also want to come out with specific examples to illustrate those strengths and weaknesses—particular articles that deal especially well or especially poorly with environmental risk. This is *not* a contest; we have no prizes to award. We will be looking for overall strengths and weaknesses, and for particular stories that best illustrate what we mean.

As you know, you will present your evaluation to an invitational conference of the state's journalists on October 4. In addition, we will write it up, together with the results of the formal content analysis, in a report to the granting agency. This in turn will become the basis for both academic and trade journal articles assessing environmental journalism, which we hope the state's media will use as a guide to self-improvement. Finally, the Environmental Risk Reporting project itself will use the results of your evaluation to help decide what research and training programs would be most fruitful in the coming years.

5. *Do you have to reach consensus?* No. Any judgment you four agree on will be very persuasive, of course. But we expect some disagreements as well, and we expect to learn from them and report them carefully.

6. *How will the evaluation process work?* We have divided the archive into six packets, and photocopied the packets so that each of you can have a complete set. The evaluation procedure will consist of alternating periods of reading and discussion. (Please see the tentative schedule.) We will ask you to take notes as you read. Your notes will constitute our record of your responses to the articles; they will also help you remember the points you want to make in your discussions with each other. Obviously, as you continue alternately reading and discussing, your perspective on the archive may change. At the end of the weekend you will have a chance to produce your individual summing–up of the strengths and weaknesses of environmental risk reporting in New Jersey.

We have done some preliminary thinking about the kinds of issues you may want to consider as you evaluate the archive. Our list of proposed standards is attached to this memo. In order to organize your note–taking and the discussions that follow, we have provided a separate page for notes on each of the standards. Thus, if a particular article triggered a comment about, say, bias, you would write the comment (and the I.D. number of the article) on the notes page dealing with objectivity and bias. The discussions will go standard by standard, not article by article. We will spend some time at the beginning of the weekend adjusting these proposed standards as you think best. New standards may also emerge during the discussions, to be used in future reading sessions. And of course any time you have a comment that doesn't fit any of the standards, make it anyway. The standards are meant as a guide, not a straitjacket.

Please make sure your comments are readable; type them if you wish. And please be sure to note the I.D. number of the article that provokes the comment.

7. *Do you have to comment on every article?* No—only those that trigger a comment.

8. *Do you have to read every article?* We think we have provided enough time to read, or at least skim, every article. If we are wildly off, we'll revise the tentative schedule as needed. But please remember that you are reading for overall strengths and weaknesses, good examples and bad examples. You need not digest every word of every article.

9. *How will the logistics work?* All discussion sessions will take place in the Seth Hoyden room. You are welcome to do your reading there, or in your own room, as you prefer. We will have dinner together Friday evening and lunch together Sunday afternoon; breakfasts are on your own; the other meals we'll decide together as we go along. There is an overnight reading packet both Friday and Saturday night; obviously it is up to you whether to work in the evening, in the early morning, or half–and–half. All this adds up to a fairly intense working weekend. If an in–room movie or a room service snack will help you endure, all expenses are on us.

10. *A note on "strengths" and "weaknesses."* Human nature being what it is, you will probably find more to criticize than to praise—but good examples are just as instructive as bad examples, and a lot easier to take. So please look consciously for environmental risk reporting that you admire. And when it comes to the reporting that you do *not* admire, please consider whether you think you have found a serious problem likely to affect the reader's understanding of environmental risk, or just a professional quibble. Point out the professional quibbles too, so reporters can learn to get them right—but try to distinguish in your notes the serious problems from the less serious ones.

Appendix C:
List of Journalists and
Non–Journalists Interviewed

Journalists

Name	Newspaper	Survey Returned+
Todd Bates	*Asbury Park Press*	no
Sandra Cummings	*Asbury Park Press*	yes
John Hudzinski	*Asbury Park Press*	yes
Pat McDaniels	*Asbury Park Press*	yes
Michael Taylor	*Asbury Park Press*	yes
Joe Donahue	*Atlantic City Press*	yes
Chris Biddle	*Burlington County Times*	yes
Leslie Snyder	*Courier–News* (Bridgewater)	yes
Judy Petsonk	*Courier–Post* (Cherry Hill)	yes
Jim Dao	*Daily Journal* (Elizabeth)	yes
Phil Garber	*Daily Record* (Morristown)	yes
Larry Hackett	*Daily Record* (Morristown) (now at *Star–Ledger*)	yes
Tom DiPiazza	*Dispatch* (Union City)	no
Elliot Goldberg	*Gloucester County Times*	yes
Lynne O'Connell	*Gloucester County Times*	yes
Pat Politano	*Herald News* (Passaic)	yes
Kent Roeder	*Herald News* (Passiac)	yes
Brad Rudin	*Herald News* (Passiac)	no
AnneMarie Cooke	*Home News* (New Brunswick)	yes
Sarah Strohmeyer	*Home News* (New Brunswick)	yes
Bob Larkins	*Jersey Journal* (Jersey City)	yes
Fred Aun	*New Jersey Herald* (Newton)	no
Donna Kenyon	*News Tribune* (Woodbridge)	yes
William Terdoslavich	*North Jersey Advance* (Dover) (formerly *Daily Advance*)	no

+One survey was returned anonymously.

*The *Vineland Times Journal* and the *Millville Daily* are owned by the same company and share reporting staff.

Journalists (Continued)

Name	Newspaper	Survey Returned[+]
Don Bennett	*Ocean County Observer*	yes
Gordon Bishop	*Star–Ledger* (Newark)	yes
Sue Epstein	*Star–Ledger* (Newark)	yes
Tom Johnson	*Star–Ledger* (Newark)	no
Jim O'Neill	*Star–Ledger* (Newark)	yes
Anita Susi	*Star–Ledger* (Newark)	yes
Bettina Boxal	*The Record* (Hackensack)	yes
Vivian Waixel	*The Record* (Hackensack)	no
Olga Wickerhauser	*The Record* (Hackensack)	no
Jane Foderaro	*The Register* (Shrewsbury)	no
Wilson Barto	*The Trentonian*	yes
Chris Blake	*Today's Sunbeam* (Salem)	no
Pat Gilbert	*Trenton Times*	no
Fran Sheehan	*Vineland Times Journal* *Millville Daily**	yes

[+] One survey was returned anonymously.

*The *Vineland Times Journal* and the *Millville Daily* are owned by the same company and share reporting staff.

Government

County

Steve Tiffinger
Bergen County Health Department

Robert Ferraiuolo
Hudson County Regional Health Commission

Harold Hershey
Middlesex County Health Department

Richard Kozub
Middlesex County Health Department
Emergency Response

Tom Mizerak
Middlesex County Health Department
Landfills

Lester Jargowsky
Monmouth County Health Department

City/Municipality

Glen Belnay
Hillsborough Township Health Department

Walter Lezynski
Jersey City Health Department

State

Joe DePierro
N.J. Department of Environmental Protection
Bureau of Emergency Response

Charlie Krauss
N.J. Department of Environmental Protection
Emergency Response Team

Jim Staples
N.J. Department of Environmental Protection
Public Information Officer

Frank Marshall
N.J. Department of Health
Emergency Response Coordinator

Harold Spedding
N.J. State Police Emergency Management

Federal

Ash Holmes
Federal Emergency Management Agency
Emergency Operations

Jim Holton
Federal Emergency Management Agency
Emergency Training

Robert Blair
Federal Emergency Management Agency
News and Information Division

Marianne Jackson
Federal Emergency Management Agency
Public Information Officer

Ann Fenn
U.S. Environmental Protection Agency
Community Relations

Robert Cibulskis
U.S. Environmental Protection Agency
Emergency Response Team

Joe Lafornara
U.S. Environmental Protection Agency
Emergency Response Team

Mike Polito
U.S. Environmental Protection Agency
Emergency Response Team

Fred Rubel
U.S. Environmental Protection Agency
Emergency Response Team

Mike Urban
U.S. Environmental Protection Agency
Emergency Response Team

Margaret Randol
U.S. Environmental Protection Agency
Public Information Officer

Linda Garczynski
U.S. Environmental Protection Agency
Superfund

Industry

Joe Caporossi
American Cyanamid
Health, Safety, Emergency Response

Joe Mayhew
Chemical Manufacturers Association
CHEMTREC

Craig Skaggs
Dupont Chemicals
Public Affairs Manager

Lawrence Norton
National Agricultural Chemicals Association

Jon DiGesu
The Chlorine Institute
Public Relations

Environmental/Community Groups

Anne Morris
Association of New Jersey Environmental Commissions

Peter Montague
Environmental Research Foundation

Mary Uva
Natural Resources Defense Council

Others

Lynda Tupling
American Red Cross
Media Coordination

David Palmer
Emergency Response Planning and Management, Inc.

Mary Ann Fowler
Reporters' Committee for Freedom of the Press
Freedom of Information Hotline

Harry Disch
Scientists' Institute for Public Information

Fred Jerome
Scientists' Institute for Public Information

Michele Demak
University of Medicine and Dentistry of New Jersey—Robert Wood
Johnson Medical School
Environmental and Occupational Health Information Program

Appendix D:
Mail Survey Form

Thanks for taking the time to talk with me. I appreciate your help and interest. As I explained over the phone, we are looking at the possibility of setting up an "environmental emergency information response team" in New Jersey. The proposed team would provide information to reporters at the scene of a spill, chemical fire, or the like. We are envisioning a mobile unit that would travel to the scene of a breaking environmental story to dispense "background" technical information where and when it was most needed. The proposed team is *not* intended to replace the emergency responders who are the best people for answering questions about; What happened? Was anyone hurt? Will people be evacuated? etc.

This feasibility study is part of a research grant to "Environmental Risk Reporting" from New Jersey's Institute for Hazardous and Toxic Waste Management. "Environmental Risk Reporting" is an ad hoc group—we're listed on the stationery—formed to do research and training on media coverage of environmental risk.

As part of this feasibility study we're doing extensive surveys of reporters, emergency response experts, and directors of emergency information programs. You can help us by filling out the enclosed questionnaire. Your comments and ideas are going to be central to this project; an "environmental emergency information response team" can only be successful if it is needed and used by reporters.

Thanks for taking the time to do this questionnaire. A stamped, addressed envelope is enclosed for returning it. If you have any questions about this project or questionnaire, please call me at 201/932-9210.

Sincerely,

Laurel Van Leer
Research Coordinator

Environmental Risk Reporting:
Survey of Reporters

Listed below are the questions you might ask or background information you might need to cover an environmental story. There are two factors we want you to consider: how important is the item to you and how difficult is it to get. Please rate each item in the following way and, *in addition* to giving each item a rating, please circle any that you currently have trouble getting an answer to.

1. The item is important *and* urgent.
2. The item is important, but not necessarily for a story.
3. Less important.
   Circle your answer if you now have trouble getting that information.

You can use the space below each question to write comments or qualifiers to your rating. Remember, the proposed team would not replace first responders, who are the best people at the scene to give information like how did it happen, was anyone hurt, etc.

I. CHEMICAL(s) INVOLVED IN INCIDENT

A. General Information
_____ 1. Name (trade and technical)
_____ 2. Use
_____ 3. Does it occur naturally in the environment?
_____   a. At what levels?
_____ 4. At what levels is it permitted in the environment or workplace?
_____ 5. If accident happened offsite, where is the chemical manufactured?
_____ 6. Is it manufactured locally?

B. Health and Environmental Effects
_____ 1. What impact, if any, does it have on human health?
_____ 2. Does it increase the likelihood of cancer?
_____   a. What type of cancer?
_____   b. What kinds of studies were done to show it's a carcinogen?
_____   c. How sure are scientists about this?
_____   d. How serious a carcinogen is it?
_____ 3. Does it increase the likelihood of genetic mutation?
_____ 4. Does it increase the likelihood of birth defects?
_____ 5. Does it cause skin or eye irritations?
_____ 6. How much does it take to be hazardous?

———— 7. What are the treatment methods after exposure?

———— 8. Effects on wildlife?

———— 9. Effects on aquatic life?

————10. Effects on plants?

————11. Is there any evidence of long term emotional or psychological effects?

————12. Can it damage property? (e.g. paint on homes and cars)?

————13. Can it damage the community's infrastructure (e.g. the biological treatment agents in sewage treatment plants)?

C. Chemical Behavior

———— 1. Is it water soluble?

———— 2. Can it get into the local water supply?

———— 3. Is it fat soluble (i.e. is it stored in human fat tissue)?

———— 4. Is it a liquid, gas or solid?

———— 5. Can it travel from the accident site?

———— 6. How can it travel from site? airborne dust? vapor? water? ground?

———— 7. Can it explode?

———— 8. Is it flammable?

———— 9. Is it a corrosive?

————10. Can it biodegrade?

————11. How long does it stay in the environment?

————12. What's the LD–50 (lethal dose that kills half the test animals)?

————13. Are there health and safety precautions I should take while covering this story?

Other information you would want to know about the chemical(s) involved (remember, the proposed team would not be providing information that is currently available from emergency responders at the scene.)

II. COMPANY OR AGENCY RESPONSIBLE

———— 1. Telephone number

———— 2. Address

———— 3. Size

———— 4. Other locations

———— 5. Night telephone number

———— 6. President's name

———— 7. Accident record

———— 8. Lawsuit record

———— 9. Are they a subsidiary of a larger company?

————10. Do they have an emergency response plan?

_____11. Who is in charge of their emergency response plan?

Other information you would want to know about the company or agency responsible?

III. SURROUNDING ENVIRONMENT

_____ 1. Is it near drinking water sources?
_____ 2. Is it near other waterways?
_____ 3. What's the local community like?
_____ 4. How many people live nearby?
_____ 5. Are there schools nearby?
_____ 6. Is it near hospitals, nursing homes or other high density institutions?
_____ 7. Is it near a major highway or airport?
_____ 8. What are the existing environmental problems in the area, if any?

Other information you would want to know about the surrounding area:

IV. LEGAL

_____ 1. What municipal government has jurisdiction over the site?
_____ 2. What laws govern the chemical in this type of event (e.g. transportation, manufacturing or storage)?
_____ 3. What permits are required?
_____ 4. What laws govern liability for this type of accident?
_____ 5. What lists is it on (e.g. EPA carcinogen; OSHA; etc.)?
_____ 6. What laws govern liability for cleanup costs?
_____ 7. Who is responsible for the cleanup?

Other legal information you would want to know?

V. How useful would you find it if the proposed team could provide you with additional names of expert sources in the New Jersey area?

_____ Enormously useful
_____ Useful
_____ Marginally useful

GENERAL COMMENTS:

Approximate number of times within the last two years that you've reported an environmental risk story (e.g. superfund site; chemical leaks and fires; EDB in foods; asbestos in schools; etc.)?

_____ less than 2
_____ 2-5
_____ 6-10
_____ 11-20
_____ over 20

What percentage of your time is spent on environmental risk?

_____ less than 10%
_____ 11-25%
_____ 26-50%
_____ over 50%

If you're not currently reporting environmental stories, but did so in the past, how often did you report an environmental story?

How useful do you think an on-site source of background information (like the one we are considering) would be to you in covering environmental risk stories?

_____ Enormously useful; would greatly improve the job I could do.
_____ Useful; I would like to have such a service available.
_____ Only marginally useful; I don't feel any special need for this service.
Please comment on your answer:

We are considering an option of a telephone "hotline" for reporters to call for the same kind of background information. Compared to an on-site service, would this be:
_____ Much less useful
_____ Somewhat less useful
_____ Slightly less useful
_____ Just as useful
_____ Even better

Please comment on your answer:

How satisfied are you with the availability of background experts on environmental risk?

_____ Very satisfied
_____ Somewhat satisfied
_____ Neutral
_____ Somewhat dissatisfied
_____ Very dissatisfied

How satisfied are you with the quality of answers these experts are able to give you?

_____ Very satisfied
_____ Somewhat satisfied
_____ Neutral
_____ Somewhat dissatisfied
_____ Very dissatisfied

How satisfied are you with the timeliness of their responses to your requests for environmental risk information?

_____ Very satisfied
_____ Somewhat satisfied
_____ Neutral
_____ Somewhat dissatisfied
_____ Very dissatisfied

What would you like us to do in order to facilitate your job of getting environmental risk information to the public?

Please complete this page so we can keep track of who has responded to our questionnaire. If you want anonymity, complete this page but _detach_ it from the rest of the questionnaire when you mail it back. (That way we'll know who has responded but not which answers are yours.)

PLEASE PRINT
Your Name _____ Newspaper _____
Address _____
Telephone _____

Appendix E:
Conference Survey Form

Conference Survey

We are considering various ways of helping reporters get background health risk information while covering breaking environmental stories.

By background health information we mean information about the potential for long and short term health effects from exposure to toxic or hazardous materials such as dioxin, pesticides, asbestos, and others.

This information may include: scientific studies determining the health risk, who agrees or disagrees with the results of these studies and why, is the chemical in a form and amount that poses a health risk, and at what levels is it legally allowable in the workplace/drinking water/food/etc.

1. Circle the letter of the statement that best describes how **YOU** feel about the need for background health risk information during a breaking environmental story.

   A. It is essential but *does not need to be provided by an independent source*. Articles already have it and reporters are not having trouble finding it.

   B. It is essential and *needs to be provided by an independent source*. Articles often lack it because it is difficult to find under deadline pressure.

   C. It is essential and available but *journalists tend not to make much use of it*. Articles often lack it because reporters and editors tend to focus on the event itself.

   D. It is *not all that important beyond the basic facts* (for example that a chemical can cause cancer.) Other aspects of the story are more important.

2. Where do you think health risk information most belongs in the coverage of a breaking environmental story? Circle the letters identifying the **TWO** answers you prefer.

   A. in the breaking story itself
   B. in a sidebar to the breaking story
   C. in a second day follow–up

    D. in an in–depth feature

3. Read the following statements describing services potentially available to journalists. Assuming **TWO** of these could be provided, which would you prefer?

MY FIRST CHOICE IS _____. MY SECOND CHOICE IS _____.

    A. A compact environmental library containing easy–to–use reference books located in my newsroom or library, and training in how to use these books efficiently.
    B. A 24–hour, year–round hotline staffed by public health experts with access to national data bases on environmental health risks.
    C. Health risk information specific to a breaking environmental story telexed or telecopied directly to my newsroom by public health experts.
    D. A van at the scene of a major breaking environmental story staffed by public health experts ready to provide background information on health risk.

Circle the letter of the title that best describes your job.

    A. Environmental reporter
    B. Municipal reporter
    C. General Assignment reporter
    D. Editor
    E. Other (explain) _____
What newspaper do you work for?

Appendix F:
Scenario Instructions and List of Participants

Participants in the Tastegood Warehouse Environmental Emergency Simulation
Invitational Symposium on Environmental Risk Reporting, October 4, 1985

Technical Panel	Role(s)
Donald Deieso Director, Division of Environmental Quality N.J. Department of Environmental Protection	emergency response team; county health officer
Bernard Goldstein Chairman, Department of Environmental and Community Medicine UMDNJ—Rutgers Medical School	Toxicologist and physician at the hospital, university and company
Michael Greenberg Co–Director, Graduate Program in Public Health UMDNJ—Rutgers Medical School	citizens; workers; local government; DEP spokesperson
Richard Magee Department of Mechanical Engineering Stevens Institute of Technology	fire department; engineer for water company, university and state
James Ross Chief, Office of Emergency Preparedness N.J. Department of Environmental Protection	emergency response team; county health officer
Peter M. Sandman Department of Journalism Rutgers University	moderator
Daniel Watts Director of Center Operations Institute for Hazardous and Toxic Waste Management New Jersey Institute of Technology	industry spokesperson
Rae Zimmerman Chair, Department of Planning School of Public Administration New York University	mayor

Directions

To Reporters

A fire begins in a warehouse at midnight on a weekday. It quickly spreads, engulfing one square city block and sending a gray plume into the air. Sounds like exploding firecrackers can be heard. The warehouse is located in a mixed industrial and residential neighborhood. The police have evacuated about 150 people who live within two blocks of the warehouse.

To Technical People

1. The warehouse is owned by the Tastegood supermarket chain.
2. It contains everything that you find in a supermarket, ranging from foods to roach killers and toilet cleaning compounds.
3. Three adjacent factories manufacture records, furniture, and batteries, which means the potential emission of vinyl chloride gases, paints and thinners, wood preservatives, formaldehydes, lead, acids, and other charming substances.
4. There is a public sewerage system in the area, which means that the public sewer plant could be endangered by contamination from substances flowing into the sewers and the treatment plant.
5. A major commuter road is located ¼ mile away.
6. A hospital and a school are located ½ mile away.

When the reporters arrive, the fire has not spread beyond the warehouse. Depending upon your role, you are free to predict that the fire is or is not likely to spread. DO NOT, however, tell reporters that it has spread or that it is under control and cannot spread. The essence of the story is a fire that is also a POSSIBLE catastrophe (under deadline—the morning's paper cannot wait). DO NOT make the catastrophe happen, and do not rule it out.

Appendix G:
Data Bases for Hotline

The following data bases have been identified as useful to journalists reporting on environmental issues. Some may be difficult to use without technical assistance.

Chemical Information Systems, Inc. (CIS)

CIS began as a collection of data bases for internal use at the United States Environmental Protection Agency. Since 1984 it has been available for public use.

FEE: $300 yearly subscription (waived for degree–granting institutions), plus variable connect time charges, $55.00 to $95.00 per hour.

The Merck Index Online ($95.00). The full text of the Merck Index, containing information on chemical use, preparation, patent status, trade names, properties, and toxicity.

Oil and Hazardous Materials Technical Assistance Data System (OHM/TADS)($55.00). Contains information on all materials considered an oil or hazardous substance by the USEPA (currently 1,334 entries). Its primary function is to provide emergency response personnel with emergency information for the identification and assessment of actual or potential dangers. Also includes general information such as drinking water standards.

Structure and Nomenclature Search System (SANSS) ($85.00). Provides CAS registry number, systemic name, synonyms, trade names and cross references for each of the over 350,000 compounds listed in the other CIS data bases.

Acute Toxicity Data from the NIOSH Registry of Toxic Effects Of Chemical Substances (RTECS) ($55.00). Provides published toxicity information and literature references for 74,184 compounds.

Federal Register Search System (FRSS) ($85.00). Provides extended abstracts of Federal Register information. Abstracts include guidelines, proposed guidelines, recommendations, standards, and non-regulatory recommendations. Also lists important dates such as when a standard will become effective and public hearing schedules.

Clinical Toxicity of Commercial Products ($85.00). Contains information on manufacture, uses, and composition of about 20,000 commercial products. Provides toxicity information on individual chemicals in each compound.

Toxic Substances Control Act Plant and Production (TSCAPP) ($55.00). Contains the non-confidential portions of 85,000 product inventory reports required by TSCA.

Chemical Carcinogenesis Research Information System (CCRIS) ($55.00). Provides tumor promotion, mutagenicity, and carcinogenicity information for 882 chemicals.

Scientific Parameters for Health and the Environment, Retrieval, and Estimation (SPHERE) ($55.00). A collection of the following data bases which together provide information to assess chemical and environmental risks:

- *DERMAL.* Provides information relating to dermal absorption (exposure through skin contact) of 655 chemicals. Also contains information on toxic effects of exposure by other routes.
- *AQUIRE.* Provides information on acute, chronic, sublethal, lethal, and bioaccumulative effects of 4,179 chemicals on fresh water and salt water aquatic life.
- *ISHOW.* Information System for Hazardous Organics in Water— provides physical and chemical information for over 5,000 substances.
- *GENETOX.* Provides mutagenicity information for 3,000 chemicals.
- *ENVIROFATE.* Describes the environmental fate (for example, transport or degradation) of 450 chemicals.

Note that a data base on risk as outlined under section 8 (e) of TSCA will soon be added to SPHERE.

Chemical Activity Status Report (CASR) ($55.00). Lists all the chemicals studied by the US Environmental Protection Agency to date. Includes study summary and EPA contact.

Industry File Index System (IFIS). Provides a summary of EPA regulations for particular industries and chemicals. Contains nearly 100 industry records and over 9,000 chemical records.

BRS/Information Technologies

FEE: One time subscription cost of $75.00, plus variable connect time charges, $19.50 to $125.00 per hour.

Hazardline ($125.00 peak time; $107.50 off–peak). A full text data base designed for hazardous emergency first responders (police, fire, first aid, etc.). Contains safety and regulatory information on over 3,000 chemicals.

Embase (EMED) ($76.00; $58.50). Provides abstracts of articles on environmental health and pollution control, from over 4,000 biomedical journals worldwide.

Pollution Abstracts (POLL) ($70.00; $52.50). Provides abstracts of international technical literature in the fields of environmental science and technology, including social and legal aspects of environmental pollution.

Kirk–Othmer Encyclopedia of Chemical Technology (KIRK) ($75.00; $31.50). The full text of the twenty–five–volume bound version of this encyclopedia is available on–line. Recognized as the most authoritative and comprehensive in the field.

Industry Data Sources (HARF) ($72.50; $55.00). Provides access to major sources of statistical and directory information for sixty–five industries.

National Technical Information Service (NTIS) ($47.00; $19.50). Provides abstracts of all government–sponsored research reports and studies, including the fields of technology, biology, medicine, health sciences, and agriculture.

Dialog Information Services, Inc.

FEE: No subscription charges; variable connect time charges, $35.00 to $138.00 per hour.

AQUALINE ($35.00). Provides information on drinking water quality, water treatment, groundwater pollution, and environmental protection from 600 periodicals and research reports.

CA SEARCH ($68.00). An on–line version of Chemical Abstracts, which contains abstracts of chemical journal articles worldwide.

Chemical Exposure ($45.00). Provides information on effects of exposure to toxic chemicals. Also includes chemical properties, CAS registry numbers, synonyms, systemic names, and study summaries.

Chemical Regulation and Guidelines System (CRGS) ($70.00). An index to federal regulatory materials on control of chemical substances. Includes federal statutes, promulgated regulations, guidelines, standards, and support documents.

Chemname, Chemsearch, Chemis ($138.00). A dictionary listing of all chemicals mentioned in *CA SEARCH*. Includes systemic names and synonyms.

Embase ($84.00). See entry under *BRS/Information Technologies.*

Energyline ($95.00). An on–line version of Energy Information Abstracts that contains 8,000 records on energy and environmental topics.

Energynet ($95.00). Provides directory–type information on almost 3,000 energy–related organizations and 8,000 people. Contains information on profit and non–profit groups and government agencies with names, addresses and telephone numbers of contact people.

Enviroline ($95.00). An index of over 5,000 international publications on environmental issues, technology, law, and chemistry.

Environmental Bibliography ($60.00). An index of over 300 periodicals covering topics such as energy, land use, health, and land and water resources.

Laborlaw ($120.00). Provides summaries of decisions and source references for many labor issues, including occupational safety and health cases since 1972.

National Technical Information Services (NTIS) ($48.00). See entry under *BRS/Information Technologies.*

Occupational Safety and Health (NIOSH) ($48.00). Contains over 100,000 citations of journal articles, monographs, and technical reports covering all aspects of occupational safety and health, including hazardous agents, unsafe workplace environments and toxicology.

Toxic Substances Control Act Initial Inventory ($45.00). Provides a non–bibliographic listing of chemicals on the TSCA inventory as of June 1, 1979, including preferred name, synonyms, and CAS registry number.

Water Resources Abstracts ($45.00). Provides abstracts of 172,000 records on topics such as water quality, pollution, and waste treatment.

Mead Data Central

FEE: No subscription charges; connect time charge of $20.00 per hour and variable search charges of $6.00 to $21.00 per hour (peak) and $3.00 to $10.50 (off–peak).

LEXIS. Contains thirty topic libraries, including energy, environment, and state court decisions. This system can be used to trace decisions, identify previous lawsuits and charges, and find federal statutes, codes, and regulations.

NEXIS. Contains 140 files of international newspapers, magazines, wire services, and newsletters covering business, finance, government, and news. This system can be searched for a range of environmental information including energy, the chemical industry, and the complete text of the Federal Register.

MEDIS. This medical service can be searched for information on cancer and the full text of several public health journals.

National Library of Medicine

FEE: No subscription charges; variable connect time charges, $45.00 to $75.00 per hour.

Chemline ($52.00 peak; $45.00 off–peak). A chemical dictionary containing records on 625,000 substances. Records include CAS registry numbers, synonyms, chemical information, and cross references to records in other NLM systems.

Toxline ($72.00; $65.00). Provides bibliographic information on the physiological and toxicological effects of drugs and other chemicals.

Toxicology Data Bank (TDB) ($75.00; $68.00). Provides approximately 4,000 peer–reviewed records for chemicals that are highly regulated, are produced in high volume, or exhibit high toxicity potential. Includes toxicity and manufacturing, environmental, occupational, and use information.

Hazardous Substances Data Bank (HSDB) ($72.00; $65.00). An expanded version of TDB covering more chemicals and focusing on environmental fate, exposure standards, regulations, monitoring, and safety precautions. The extra information is scientifically reviewed but not as completely as in the TDB system.

Registry of Toxic Effects of Chemical Substances (RTECS) ($55.00; $48.00). See entry under *Chemical Information Systems, Inc.*

Newsnet, Inc.

FEE: $180.00 annual subscription charge; variable connect time charges, $18.00 to $24.00 per hour.

Provides the full text of 300 newsletters in many fields, including law, energy, the chemical industry, and the environment.

Information Services

BRS/Information Technologies
1200 Route 7
Latham, New York 12110
518-738-1161 or 800-227-5277

Chemical Information Systems, Inc.
7215 York Road
Baltimore, Maryland 21212
301-321-8440

Dialog Information Services, Inc.
3460 Hillview Avenue
Palo Alto, California 94304
415-858-3785 or 800-227-1927

Mead Data Central
3939 Springboro Pike
P.O. Box 933
Dayton, Ohio 45401
513-865-6800

National Library of Medicine
Office of Inquiries and Publications Management
8600 Rockville Pike
Bethesda, Maryland 20209
301-496-6193 or 301-496-1131

Newsnet, Inc.
945 Haverford Road
Bryn Mawr, Pennsylvania 19010
800-345-1301

Appendix H:
Cost Information

Mobile Environmental Risk Information Team

First Year	Description	Capital	Salary
Answering Service	24–hour availability, capable of screening emergency calls	$1,000.00	–
Van	Medicoach Goldstar—exterior storage space, two frequency controlled batteries, 4 KW generator, Triplight PV 1000 frequency controlled power inverter, mounted chair and table for computer operator, mounted shelves and cabinets	$50,000.00	–
Van Accessories	tool kit, clock, NJ maps, folding chairs and tables, chalkboard, highway cones or stanchions, standard office supplies	$1,000.00	–
Multiple Output Box	15–channel, multi–pin output capability	$450.00	–
Personal Computer with Modem and Printer	IBM PC 5150, includes Hayes Smartmodem, 256 K memory, color adaptors for screen, can also serve as word processor with Brother Dual Mode Printer	$3,930.00	–
Telecopier	Xerox TC–295, compatible with G–1, G–2 telecopiers	$2,650.00	–
Photocopier	Canón PC–20, eight copies per minute, small, portable, durable, lightweight	$800.00	–
Typewriter	Sharp 3250, lightweight, durable, compact, rechargeable batteries	$400.00	–
Safety Gear	goggles, rainwear, first aid kit, hard hats, jumpsuits, general purpose respirators, gloves, boots, ear protection	$600.00	–

Item	Description		
Cellular Phones (three)	Harris Alpha Custom Phones, for data transmission and two–way communication system	$7,200.00	–
Reference Manuals	"Merck Index," "Dangerous Properties of Industrial Materials," "Registry of Toxic Effects," "Condensed Chemicals Dictionary," and others (see Appendix G)	$700.00	–
Cassette Recorder	Marantz PMD 220, durable, good mike, excellent audio quality	$400.00	–
Public Address System	Paso II system, microphone, speaker, cabinet	$400.00	–
Safety Courses (two)	Red Cross CPR and First Aid, Analysis of Hazardous Chemical Emergencies (held at Rutgers, run by DEP and State Police)	$200.00	–
Data bases (start-up)	BRS Information Technologies, Chemical Information Systems, Inc., Dialog Information System, Mead Data Central, National Library of Medicine, Newsnet, Inc. (see Appendix G)	$555.00	–
Data base Training Programs (four)	recommended because information organization varies among vendors	$400.00	–
Data base Use	40 hrs. at $75/hr.	$3,000.00	–
Miscellany	supplies, photocopies, etc.	$7,000.00	–
Public Health Specialist	M.A., Ph.D. in Public Health, Toxicology, Chemistry or related field. Will be on call 24-hours per day, 365 days per year, and be required to go to the site of a breaking environmental story no more than ten times per year to provide reporters with background health and environmental information. Will be proficient at data base searching and have good communication skills.	–	$6,000.00
Public Information Emergency Response Assistant	B.A., B.S. Will be on call 24-hours per day, 365 days per year, and be required to go to the site of a breaking environmental story no more than ten times per year and assist Public Health Specialist. Will provide secretarial and support functions on site. Will be proficient in data base searching and have good communication skills.	–	$4,000.00

(Continued on next page)

Mobile Environmental Risk Information Team (Continued)

Description	Capital	Salary
First Year		
Full-Time Staff Person	–	$15,000.00
Organize/Publicize/Manage System	–	$10,000.00
Fringe Benefits at 25% of salaries	–	$8,750.00
TOTAL FIRST YEAR	$80,685.00 +	$43,750.00

Description	Capital	Salary
Following Years		
Answering Service	$1,000.00	–
Data bases (annual fees)	$480.00	–
Equipment Maintenance, etc. at 20% of cost	$14,000.00	–
Data base Use (40 hrs. at $75/hr.)	$3,000.00	–
Miscellany	$4,000.00	–
Public Health Specialist	–	$6,000.00
Public Information Emergency Response Assistant	–	$4,000.00
Full-Time Staff Person	–	$15,000.00
Organize/Publicize/Manage System	–	$5,000.00
Fringe Benefits (at 25% of salaries)	–	$7,500.00
TOTAL FOLLOWING YEARS	$22,480.00 +	$37,500.00

24–Hour Hotline

First Year	Description	Capital	Salary
Personal Computer with Modem and Printer	IBM PC 5150, includes Hayes Smartmodem, 256 K memory, color adaptors for screen, can also serve as word processor with Brother Dual Mode Printer	$3,930.00	–
Reference Manuals	"Merck Index," "Dangerous Properties of Industrial Materials," "Registry of Toxic Effects," "Condensed Chemicals Dictionary," and others (see Appendix G)	$700.00	–
Telephones (three)	two AT&T 10-extension phones and one AT&T standard phone	$1,230.00	–
Call Sequencer (8–line)	a two–minute continuous loop message, handles overflow calls until staff member is free	$5,442.00	–
Answering Service	24–hour availability, capable of screening emergency calls	$1,000.00	–
Data bases (start–up)	BRS Information Technologies, Chemical Information Systems, Inc., Dialog Information System, Mead Data Central, National Library of Medicine, Newsnet, Inc. (see Appendix G)	$555.00	–
Data base Training Programs (eight)	recommended because information organization varies among vendors	$800.00	–
Data base Use	10 hrs. x 52 wks. at $75/hr.	$39,000.00	–
Office		$6,000.00	–
Miscellany	supplies, photocopies, etc.	$7,000.00	–
Public Health Specialists (two at $35,000/ea.)	M.A., Ph.D. in Public Health, Toxicology, Chemistry or related field. Will be on call 24-hours per day, 365 days per year, including a 35–hour per week office shift, to answer reporters' questions on health and environmental risks. Will be proficient at data base searching and have good communication skills.	–	$70,000.00

(Continued on next page)

24–Hour Hotline (Continued)

First Year	Description	Capital	Salary
Data Retrieval Specialists (two at $30,000/ea.)	M.A. in Computer or Library Science. Will be on call 24-hours per day, 365 days per year, including a 35-hour per week office shift, to assist Public Health Specialist. Primary responsibility will be to conduct information searches. Should have good communication skills.	–	$60,000.00
Secretary	Will provide clerical support as needed. Tasks will include typing, correspondence, data transmission, logging calls.	–	$15,000.00
Organize/Publicize/Manage System		–	$10,000.00
Fringe Benefits	at 25% of salaries		$38,750.00
TOTAL FIRST YEAR		$65,657.00 +	$193,750.00

Following Years		Capital	Salary
Answering Service		$1,000.00	–
Data bases (annual fees)		$480.00	–
Equipment Maintenance, etc. at 20% of cost		$2,600.00	–
Data base Use (10 hrs. x 52 wks. at $75/hr.)		$39,000.00	–
Office		$6,000.00	–
Miscellany		$7,000.00	–
Public Health Specialists (2 at $35,000)		–	$70,000.00
Data Retrieval Specialists (2 at $30,000)		–	$60,000.00
Secretary		–	$15,000.00

		Capital	Salary
Organize/Publicize/Manage System		–	$5,000.00
Fringe Benefits (at 25% of salaries)		–	$37,500.00
TOTAL FOLLOWING YEARS		$56,080.00 +	$187,500.00

Environmental Risk Wire Service

First Year	Description	Capital	Salary
Personal Computer with Modem and Printer	IBM PC 5150, includes Hayes Smartmodem, 256 K memory, color adaptors for screen, can also serve as word processor with Brother Dual Mode Printer	$3,930.00	–
Reference Manuals	"Merck Index," "Dangerous Properties of Industrial Materials," "Registry of Toxic Effects," "Condensed Chemicals Dictionary," and others (see Appendix G)	$700.00	–
Automatic Dialer	Panasonic dialer with 32-number memory, compatible with telecopiers, last number redial feature, battery backup memory	$112.00	–
Telephones	two standard phones, one for data transmission, one for phone calls	$200.00	–
Photocopier	Canon PC–20, durable, lightweight	$795.00	–
Telecopier	Xerox TC–295, compatible with G–1, G–2 telecopiers	$2,645.00	–
Data bases (start–up)	BRS Information Technologies, Chemical Information Systems, Inc., Dialog Information System, Mead Data Central, National Library of Medicine, Newsnet, Inc. (see Appendix G)	$555.00	–
Data base Training Programs (four)	recommended because information organization varies among vendors	$400.00	–

(Continued on next page)

Environmental Risk Wire Service (Continued)

First Year	Description	Capital	Salary
Data base Use	20 hrs. at $75/hr.	$1,500.00	–
Miscellany	supplies, photocopies, etc.	$5,000.00	–
Health Education Specialist	Ph.D. in Public Health, Toxicology, Chemistry or related field. Will be on call 24-hours per day, 365 days per year. Will write from five to twenty manuscripts on environmental risk topics as they arise.	–	$10,000.00
Secretary	Will provide clerical support as needed. Tasks will include typing, correspondence, data transmission, logging calls.	–	$15,000.00
Organize/Publicize/Manage System		–	$10,000.00
Fringe Benefits	at 25% of salaries	–	$8,750.00
Consultants	20 at $200/ea.	–	$4,000.00
Artists	20 at $200/ea.	–	$4,000.00
TOTAL FIRST YEAR		$15,837.00 +	$51,750.00

Following Years		Capital	Salary
Data bases (annual fees)		$480.00	–
Equipment Maintenance, etc. at 20% of cost		$1,680.00	–
Data base Use (20 hrs. at $75/hr.)		$1,500.00	–
Miscellany		$5,000.00	–
Health Education Specialist		–	$10,000.00

	Salary
Secretary	$15,000.00
Organize/Publicize/Manage System	$5,000.00
Fringe Benefits (at 25% of salaries)	$7,500.00
Consultants (20 at $200/ea.)	$4,000.00
Artists (20 at $200/ea.)	$4,000.00
TOTAL FOLLOWING YEARS	$8,660.00 + $45,500.00

Environmental Risk Library

	Description	Capital	Salary
First Year			
Reference Books (26 sets at $500)		$13,000.00	–
"NIOSH Guide"	health hazards, symptoms, list of chemicals and forms, incompatibilities, personal protection, sanitation, exposure limits		
"Merck Index"	physical and toxicity data on 10,000 entries		
"Registry of Toxic Effects"	physical properties and literature references for 145,000 substances		
"Condensed Chemicals Dictionary"	physical properties, hazards, industrial uses		
"Handbook of Toxic & Hazardous Chemicals & Carcinogens"	concise safety information on 800 hazardous chemicals, EPA priority substances		

(Continued on next page)

Environmental Risk Library (Continued)

First Year	Description	Capital	Salary
"Dangerous Properties of Industrial Materials"	physical properties and hazard analysis on 18,000 common substances	$4,000.00	–
Training Conference	rooms, instructor fees, audio–visual materials, instructor's copy of reference manuals	–	$8,000.00
Miscellany	supplies, photocopies, etc.	$3,000.00	–
Organize/Publicize/Manage System		–	$2,000.00
Fringe Benefits	at 25% of salaries	–	$2,000.00
Consultants		–	$2,000.00
TOTAL FIRST YEAR		$20,000.00 +	$12,000.00

Following Years		Capital	Salary
Training Conference (biennial)		$2,000.00	–
Replacement Books (at 20% of original cost)		$2,600.00	–
Miscellany		$1,500.00	–
Organize/Publicize/Manage System		–	$4,000.00
Fringe Benefits (at 25% of salaries)		–	$1,000.00
Consultants		–	$1,000.00
TOTAL FOLLOWING YEARS		$6,100.00 +	$6,000.00

Environmental Risk Press Kit

First Year	Description	Capital	Salary
Kits	200 at $25/ea.	$5,000.00	–
Reprint Permissions		$2,000.00	–
Miscellany	supplies, photocopies, etc.	$5,000.00	–
Research and Writing		–	$10,000.00
Organize/Publicize/ Manage System		–	$2,000.00
Evaluation		–	$4,000.00
Fringe Benefits	at 25% of salaries	–	$4,000.00
Consultants		–	$4,000.00
TOTAL FIRST YEAR		$12,000.00 +	$24,000.00

Following Years		Capital	Salary
Kits (100 at $25/ea.)		$2,500.00	–
Reprint Permissions		$1,000.00	–
Miscellany		$2,500.00	–
Research and Writing		–	$5,000.00
Organize/Publicize/ Manage System		–	$2,000.00
Fringe Benefits (at 25% of salaries)		–	$1,750.00
Consultants		–	$2,000.00
TOTAL FOLLOWING YEARS		$6,000.00 +	$10,750.00